Getting Lucky

Answers to Nearly Every Lottery Question You Can Ask

Ben E. Johnson, Ph.D.

Bonus Books, Inc., Chicago

98   97   96   95   94   5   4   3   2   1

Library of Congress Catalog Card Number: 94-78843

International Standard Book Number: 1-56625-016-1

Bonus Books, Inc.
160 East Illinois Street
Chicago, Illinois 60611

Cover design by Ken Toyama

Printed in the United States of America

For Elsa.
Talk about getting lucky . . . !
I got lucky when we met
and really *lucky when you married me.*

Contents

Acknowledgements

With this book, as with each book I write, I owe an affectionate thank you to my wife, Elsa, who freed me to write, who faithfully and with great sacrifice of her time assisted with the word processing chores, and who provided a lottery player's perspective on *Getting Lucky*.

I am grateful to all those staff members at state lottery headquarters in 36 lottery states and the District of Columbia who regularly send me information and keep me updated concerning lottery happenings, winners, new games, and other important lottery information found in these pages.

A special thanks to Jane Jordan Browne, my literary agent, who had the professional insight to present this book idea to Bonus Books. The staff at Bonus Books was a pleasure to work with.

And finally, to all of the readers of my weekly newspaper column, "The Lottery Column," and my columns in *LottoWorld Magazine* and *WIN Magazine*, thank you for all the letters and questions over the past six years. Your questions made this book possible.

Introduction

GETTING LUCKY: Answers to Nearly Every Lottery Question You Can Ask is a book about exactly that—how to increase your chances of getting lucky playing the lottery. But it is more than that.

GETTING LUCKY is a collection of frequently asked questions that the 100 million weekly lottery players in this country wish they had answers for. Lottery players have lots of questions—but they don't know who to ask in order to get answers. They believe that if they only had their questions answered, those answers would give them an edge, a way to beat the seemingly overwhelming odds against winning the lottery. And they are correct. Players have questions about the different lottery games, about lottery winners (and losers), about whether or not to try a winning "system" they have heard or read about. They have questions about the many "offers" that are made to lottery players that somehow sound very much like scams. They have questions about how things work in different lottery states, what the rules and regulations are for different games, and wonder just what the truth is about some lottery story they heard that sounds unbelievable.

Thousands of players have questions—the same questions

Thousands of lottery players have these unanswered questions, and not surprisingly, many of the questions are the same. Since 1987, I have been writing a weekly syndicated newspaper column, "The Lottery Column," answering as many of these questions as possible. Unfortunately, it is impossible to answer more than three or four questions in each column, thereby leaving most of the questions unanswered. **GETTING LUCKY** collects the most frequently asked of these questions and answers them. It is full of answers to questions about lottery rules, facts, procedures, the different lottery games, winners, number picking systems, mysterious lottery happenings, and much more. In fact, I suspect you will not be able to raise a lottery question that is not answered in the pages of this book.

If your question isn't answered in this book . . .

There is a very slight possibility that you may come up with a question that is not addressed in this book. If that happens, send your question to me at P.O. Box G, Bradenton Beach, Florida 34217, and I'll try to answer it for you.

And one more thing

One last point. Every attempt has been made to bring you the most current, up-to-the-moment information in every area. Unfortunately, things change so rapidly in state lotteries that in a few relatively minor areas, a number, a date, a name may have changed between the time this book was printed and the time you read it. If you become aware of a change that needs to be made in this book, please feel free to drop me a note and let me know what it is. Your helpfulness is appreciated.

Here's hoping you get lucky. May the numbers be with you.

Ben E. Johnson

PART I

Help Me Pick Some
Winning Numbers!

A Florissant, Missouri, housewife plucked $100,000 out of a hat when she had her two sons, ages 10 and 12, draw numbers out of a hat filled with numbered pieces of paper. The numbers they drew won.

James Ford of Belleville, Michigan, put numbers on pieces of paper, folded them and threw them on the floor. He let his cat sniff the pieces and the first six the cat sniffed, James played. He won $732,949.

Phil Golden of Grand Rapids, Michigan, numbered lima beans from 1 to 44, put them in a jar, and then chose six with his eyes closed. He won $11.2 million.

Terry Showalter of East Detroit, Michigan, won $5,055,996 when he played the numbers of his favorite Detroit Tigers' uniforms.

Ronnie Jonason of Bangor, Maine, won $2,173,504 when he found an old non-winning lotto ticket that his friend had left at his house. Ronnie played the same numbers and won.

Should I play numbers composed of birthdates or use quick pick?

Q: Is it a better idea to use my own numbers composed of family birthdates or to use the lottery computer's randomly selected numbers when I play lotto? And don't tell me that any set of numbers is just as likely to win as any other set of numbers, because I don't believe it.

A: Sorry, but you are going to hear it again. No higher power is at work behind the scenes determining which lotto numbers are going to be drawn. It is pure chance at work. Therefore, "any set of numbers is just as likely to win as any other set of numbers."

However, having said that, I would also like to say that I favor computerized random selection as the best way to keep from sharing your winnings if your numbers do happen to be drawn. The problem with "your" numbers, which are arrived at by using family birthdates, is that they are probably the same birthdates being used by many other players to determine their lotto numbers. If those numbers do happen to win, you'll share with all other people who used those same numbers. Chances are that the lottery's computer-generated random numbers will always have fewer people using the same numbers.

Even state lotteries recommend computerized random number selection as the best way to play. On the back of the New York State Lotto brochure there is this paragraph: "Many Lotto players are betting on several of the same number patterns. You should know that Lotto payoffs are parimutuel, and if a commonly played pattern were to hit, even a big Lotto jackpot would have to be split into a lot of small prizes. Lotto winning numbers are selected at random, and selecting your numbers randomly is the best because they are more likely to be unique and insure a bigger payoff if your numbers win."

What is the "dead relative" system for picking lotto numbers?

Q: I have a neighbor who has come up with a rather bizarre number picking system that I bet you've never heard of. She comes from a big family that has been living in this area for nearly five generations, and she has lots of ancestors buried in local cemeteries and has done tombstone rubbings of most of their gravestones. Some of her ancestors were very lucky (one struck gold in the 1800s) and some of them were considerably less lucky (two of them were hanged for horse stealing), but she hopes they will combine their luck to help her win. She says that since the numbers she uses each week don't really make much difference to her, she has decided to use the birth- and death-dates from different ancestor gravestones as the numbers she plays in our lotto game. She has told each of these ancestors (she says . . .) that she will buy a new headstone for the ancestor's grave who provides her with the winning lotto numbers. What do you think? Is this a great system or what?

A: I do like your friend's system, but I have heard of other people already using it, although not many people have won. One who did was Willie Henderson of Birmingham, Alabama. He recently won a $100,000 Powerball prize by using the birth- and deathdates from his father's grave.

Another winner, Rhonda Starling, used deathdates of loved ones last year to pick the winning numbers in the West Virginia Cash 25 game. She said, "I tried everything else. So this time I used the deathdates of my brothers, sisters-in-law, aunts and my mother. All I can say is they must have been watching over me."

Has anyone won playing the numbers found in fortune cookies?

Q: I was tickled by reading about the fortune cookies given out in Oriental restaurants that have lottery numbers in them. I'm curious, has anybody won using the numbers?

A: Yes, a couple of people have won lottery jackpots using the number combinations they found inside fortune cookies. Apparently the practice of putting lottery numbers in fortune cookies is becoming a widespread practice among fortune cookie manufacturers. People seem to give more credibility to the numbers that are inside the cookie simply because it is a "fortune" cookie, and thus they are willing to play the numbers.

Many lottery players have stated that the messages inside fortune cookies have turned out to be omens of good luck. This was the case recently for an Indianapolis, Indiana, man and his girlfriend. Walter Bush, 49, said the message inside his cookie foretold "fast financial turns" in his immediate future. His companion's cookie predicted that "someone dear to her" was going to become financially stable. The next day Bush won $11 million in the Indiana Powerball game.

A few days ago, my wife and I received fortune cookies with the Chinese take-out we brought home. Sure enough, inside were two slips of paper. On one side of the slips were these truisms: "You have an ability to sense and know higher truth," and "You have an active mind and a keen imagination." Both these statements were clearly true. On the back of these slips were two lottery number combinations: 23 48 06 32 13 41 and 14 26 22 32 11 45. Readers of this book are welcome to use these "lucky" numbers. And, if you win, don't forget who gave you the winning numbers.

What do you think about a "biblical" number picking system?

Q: I read an article the other day which said that people can win the lottery by playing certain numbers that appear in the

Bible. I would like to have your opinion of this. Apparently some person did a computerized analysis of the numbers that appear in the Bible and has concluded that God will reward with lottery jackpots those who play the numbers 3, 7, 10, 12, 27, 29, 30, 40, 49, 50, along with their birthdays. Our birthday is special because it is the day on which a person is given life and life is the greatest gift of all. This article said that the numbers 7 and 40 should be used in all lottery combinations because they are the most widely used numbers in the Holy Scriptures, and spiritual people who live by God's Word must use these numbers. The article actually says, "Statistics show that these 10 numbers, in addition to the varying digits of the player's birthday, will give you a much greater chance of winning." What do you think about this?

A: Not much. Besides, I never trust anyone who says, "statistics show" in order to prove a point, especially when they say it in a supermarket tabloid article as is the case here. That phrase, "statistics show," is usually only said when there is little if any proof for what is being said as a fact.

It is obvious that the man who did this "computerized analysis" of numbers in the Bible knows nothing about winning lottery numbers. The truth is that in the history of North American lotteries, this guy's 10 biblical numbers (and a birthday!) have not been any luckier—have not won more often—than any of the other non-biblical numbers. If he had taken the time to check out which numbers have won in every lottery state, and that information is readily available, he would have found that no numbers, biblical or otherwise, win more often than any other numbers.

And just because a computerized analysis identifies which numbers appear most often in the Bible, why should we assume that those numbers now qualify as lucky lottery numbers? My knowledge of the Bible may be a bit limited, but I don't remember any place in the Bible where we are instructed about which lottery numbers to play.

As an editor friend of mine points out, why not do the same thing with other sacred writings, or even the *Bhagavad Gita?* A computer analysis of numbers in these works might be very interesting, but they would be just as worthless for finding winning lottery numbers.

Be skeptical of anyone who claims to be able to tell you winning lottery numbers, especially anyone who claims to have divine insight.

Is there a winning number picking system for pick-4 games?

Q: Have you heard of any systems for picking winning numbers in our pick-4 game?

A: I have heard of pick-4 winners who have used parts of Social Security numbers, street addresses, the second part of telephone numbers, and license plate numbers. One woman played her dog's birthday. He was born in November 1980, so she played 1180, which came up a winner. One woman won with the numbers 3717, her age and her daughter's age. But have I heard of any winning pick-4 "systems"? No.

Why not play the first six numbers on the play slip?

Q: Last week, and at nearly the last possible moment, I found myself standing in a convenience store trying to decide which numbers to play. I had left my list of usual numbers at home and the drawing was just a few minutes away. So, in desperation, I marked the first six numbers—1, 2, 3, 4, 5, 6—and handed in the play slip to the clerk. I felt a bit silly, but after all, you've said it many times, "any six numbers have an equal

chance of winning as any other six numbers," so why not pick
the first six on the sheet?

A: I think you made a bad choice of numbers, even though
it is true that those numbers could have won just as easily as
any other set of numbers. Your choice was bad because, unfortunately, you weren't the only lottery player choosing those
numbers. The numbers 1-2-3-4-5-6 are one of the most popular number combination choices in every state lottery. For this
reason, it's not a good bet to make. If you'd won, you would
have had to split the jackpot with a huge number of other
winners.

In the Maryland Lottery, a relatively small lottery, those six
numbers are played on the average of 3200 times for each
weekly drawing. Think of winning a grand prize with those
numbers and having to share with over 3000 other winners! In
September of 1990, Florida had a $106 million jackpot won by
six players. Each winner received about $17 million. For that
same jackpot, over 52,000 players played the number 1-2-3-4-5-
6! If those numbers had been drawn, 52,000 winners would
have shared the jackpot. Each winner would have taken home
a one-time, lump-sum payment of about $8.

Why do so many lottery players choose this combination?
Convenience. As was the case with you, it's fast, and they
don't have to do any thinking. When you have to choose six
lotto numbers in a rush, it's much better to use the lotto
computer's quick pick system. It provides a random spread of
numbers and usually results in a much larger payoff (because
of little or no sharing with other winners) if you win.

Should I play the lotto numbers that I dream?

**Q: I think I've been playing the lottery too much. I've started
to dream about picking winning numbers in three different
dreams in the past two weeks. Most of the time I forget my**

dreams as soon as I wake up, but not my number picking dreams. Although these dream numbers are different in each dream, I actually have remembered which numbers I picked in my dreams. Do you think I should play these dream numbers? My family thinks I'm crazy.

A: Your family may be right.

But don't let that dissuade you from playing your "dream numbers." They have just as good a chance of winning as numbers picked any other way. Besides, what have you got to lose? Play the numbers, and if you win, you can rub your family's nose in the fact for many years to come. If your numbers lose, tell everyone you used the lottery's quick pick system to select your numbers.

You wouldn't be the first player to dream lottery numbers and then win when you played them. Many other lottery players over the past several years have dreamed lottery numbers and have won playing them. Take the case of Ronald Jennings of Virginia.

A few years ago, shortly after midnight on October 19, 1991, four numbers appeared to Ronald Jennings in a dream. When he awoke, he wrote the numbers on a matchbook. He, too, wondered if he should play them. He felt a little silly even thinking about it.

But, after work the next day, he stopped at a market to buy two pick-4 tickets and wagered $4 on his "dream numbers." He wagered $2 on the numbers in exact order, and $2 on the same numbers in any order. The following day, while working at the post office, Ronald told his co-workers what had happened. Everyone had a good laugh. A little later, someone checked the lottery's winning numbers for the Pick 4, then brought him the news. You guessed it. His numbers had come up in exact order. That meant that he won with both his exact-order wager and his any-order wager. Ronald won $10,800 with his dream numbers.

Why can't you buy all possible number combinations?

Q: You have said that it was impossible for someone to buy all the possible lotto number combinations for a drawing, even if they had enough money to do so. Why? If you had the money, why couldn't you buy every possible number combination, especially if the size of the jackpot made the effort worthwhile? When a state's jackpot goes over $100 million, it would seem like a good idea in order to guarantee a win. When California's Lotto jackpot hit $118 million, I certainly would have tried it if I'd had the money.

A: There are two reasons why what you are suggesting is a really bad idea.

The first reason has to do with return on investment. In order to purchase every possible number combination for California's giant $118 million jackpot you would have needed to purchase nearly 23 million different number combinations to guarantee that you got the winning one, because that's how many different possible number combinations there were in that game. If you remember, there were 10 winners of that jackpot who had to share it; you would have made 11. That means you each would have received approximately $10 million spread out over 20 years. You would have spent $23 million to win $10 million. That's a bad investment.

The second reason has to do with the sheer impossibility of purchasing that many tickets for a single drawing. Assuming you could write 500 number combinations on a single sheet of paper—so that you could keep track of which numbers you had purchased—it would take over 43,000 sheets of paper to list all 23 million number combinations. By the way, most state lotteries have now prohibited players from using mechanical or computerized marking of play slips. They must be marked by hand. Also, if you could get the 4,600,000 play slips necessary—five number combinations to a play slip—it would take over four years, about 50 months, to fill out the play slips, assuming one person filled out two play slips per minute, 24 hours a day, which is impossible. If you wanted to fill out the slips in a single eight-hour day, you would need to ask the help of 4,500 of your closest friends. And then, after you got the play slips filled out, it would take one terminal over 300 days to process all the play slips, assuming the terminal did nothing but put the slips through at the rate of one every five seconds, 18 hours a day, seven days a week. Here again is another problem: state lotteries now prohibit one person from tying up a terminal for long periods (more than 10 minutes) at a time.

Got the idea? It's not a good idea.

What is partitioning, and how does it help you win?

Q: Can you tell me what "partitioning" is and why it works?

A: First, like every other lottery number selection "system," it doesn't work—except perhaps occasionally when the luck of the draw may give the impression that partitioning determined the winning numbers in advance. I've said it many times before, but it still needs repeating: there is no way to determine winning lottery numbers in advance—absolutely no way at all. Every set of numbers played always has exactly the same chance of winning as every other set of numbers.

Now having said that, let me also say that playing a system of some sort, such as partitioning, can add substantial interest to the act of selecting numbers, and besides, numbers selected this way certainly don't stand any *worse* chance of winning than numbers selected randomly or any other way.

Partitioning theory says that half of the numbers in a draw will be in the upper half of the number field and half in the lower half of the field. In addition, half of the numbers will be odd and half will be even. This means that "partitioners" have four groups of numbers from which they may select their numbers for each drawing: lower half and odd, lower half and even, upper half and odd, upper half and even.

A person using partitioning theory who was playing the 6/49 game might use a 2-1-1-2 formula for determining numbers: two numbers selected from the odd numbers from 1 to 25, one number selected from the even numbers from 2 to 24, one number selected from the odd numbers from 27 to 49, and two numbers selected from the even numbers from 26 to 50. Got the idea?

Some players who use partitioning say that they use it just to keep their numbers spread out and not all selected from the low numbers or all from the high numbers. But, don't forget, all low numbers and all high numbers sometimes win too.

What is the "three up and three across" method of picking numbers?

Q: Can you tell me about the "three up and three across" method for picking winning lotto numbers? Apparently several jackpot winners in different states have won using this system, and I'd like to give it a try.

A: You are correct, the "three up and three across" system has worked a few times, but there really isn't much of a "system" to it.

Robert Yniguez is the most recent winner that I know of to win using this number picking technique. On January 22, 1992, Yniguez won a $5.5 million Arizona jackpot. How did Yniguez do it? Simple. He was in a hurry and simply marked three numbers straight up on the play slip and then marked three numbers straight across. Was there any certain place to start when marking the play slip, or any specific number to include? No. Yniguez says that he just closes his eyes, puts the pencil point down on the play slip and that is where he begins. He then marks "three up and three across." It seems to me that this is just about as good a "system" as any other number selection method I have heard of.

Am I guaranteed to win if I don't change the numbers I play?

Q: How's this for a guaranteed way to win the lottery? Pick your set of numbers, don't change them, and play them every drawing.

If it is true that random selection is the operating principle behind winning lottery number selection, and that over a long enough period of time every set of numbers will eventually be drawn, it stands to reason that if I play the same lotto numbers each drawing, eventually my combination of numbers will be drawn as the winning numbers. Is that correct?

A: That's correct, but it might be a very long time if you are waiting for this to happen in lotto. There are just too many different possible number combinations to get through. For example, in a 6/49 lotto, there are 14 million different number combinations. If a different set of numbers is picked each week—and so far, the same set of lotto numbers has never been drawn a second time in any state—it would take 14 million weeks (about 270,000 years!) before each set of numbers was drawn once.

But there is hope for you—and your "guaranteed" winning system—if you play the same set of numbers in the pick-3 games. Since you have fewer number combinations to pick from, only 1000, probably all the number combinations in this game will be drawn at least once in your lifetime. Already, several states have had every number combination selected in their pick-3 games. The New Jersey Pick-3 game is the latest lottery game in the country to finally have drawn all of the possible number combinations that it can draw. Number 394 was the last 3-digit number not yet drawn and it hit on Monday, July 12,

1993, after 18 years of play. It was the 5,877th pick-3 drawing. The first pick-3 drawing was May 22, 1975.

Any advice for starting a lottery pool?

Q: We are starting a neighborhood lottery pool and are wondering if there is one important piece of advice that you think we should keep in mind?

A: I guess if you are limiting me to just one important piece of advice it would be this: when the tickets are purchased each week, the ticket purchaser should make photocopies of all the tickets and give each pool member a copy so that after the drawing each person could check the numbers and know immediately whether the pool had won. This could keep problems from developing at a later point.

Ownership of a Virginia Lotto ticket worth $9 million is currently being disputed by several people in a pool in North Carolina. One side of the dispute claims that the group purchased the winning ticket; the other side claims that one person (the person who purchased the ticket) owns the ticket. A judge in Virginia issued a restraining order, prohibiting the Virginia Lottery from making any payments on the ticket until the legal system decides the fate of the 20 annual payments of more than $450,000 each. If group members had been given photocopies of the tickets when purchased, there would be no question about ownership.

Should I join a lottery pool?

Q: Is it better to be a member of a lottery pool and have a greater chance of winning but have to share any winnings with other pool members, or is it better to play by myself, betting the same amount of money I would have contributed to the pool, not be able to play as many number combinations each week, but keep the whole thing if I win?

A: It really depends on your personal philosophy. My philosophy is that a little is better than nothing so I would vote for the pool because pools increase the chances of winning by purchasing more tickets than I could afford by myself.

And pools are winning all the time. Eleven maintenance and security workers at a Cincinnati office tower decided to pool the money they had each been spending for lotto tickets every week. After only five weeks the pool won a $12 million Ohio jackpot. Each of the pool members will receive $32,097 a year for the next 26 years.

On the other hand, Indianapolis resident George Thomas was part of a 10-member lotto pool at work that customarily bought $100 tickets in the 6/44 lotto cash game each week. But when the 39-year-old man missed a day of work last March, the pool dumped him, buying only $90 worth of tickets. Thomas decided to buy his own $10 worth of tickets—and won $2 million! His lump-sum check totaled $1.6 million. "They kicked me out, but I'm glad," Thomas said. "I'm very glad now."

How should a pool pick its numbers?

Q: A few of us at work are forming a lottery pool and putting in $5 a week to play our state lotto game. We've been having a bit of controversy about how to pick the numbers we will play each week. Most of the group wants to use special numbers composed of birthdays and anniversaries and so forth, but I

would like to use random numbers selected by the lottery quick pick method. What do you say?

A: First of all, let me remind you of what I have said many times: Any set of numbers that you use, whether they are lucky numbers or randomly selected ones, have exactly the same chance of winning as any other set of numbers. So, in terms of chances of winning, it doesn't matter how you select the numbers. But, in terms of how much you keep if your numbers are the winners, that's a different story. Many lottery players use and play numbers each week based on birthdays, anniversaries and so on. And many of these players are using the same numbers as hundreds or even thousands of other players. The chances of your special numbers also being someone else's special numbers are very high. Thus, the likelihood of having to share the jackpot with a number of other winners when you play lucky numbers is much greater than if you use random selection. If I win I don't want to share, so I recommend lottery computer quick pick.

So, what should your group do? Why not do both? Let those who want to use lucky numbers use them and let those who want random selection use the quick pick method. If each member of the pool contributes $5 a week, then each member can choose five sets of numbers any way he or she pleases. Those numbers can then be put on play slips and those play slips used every week after that in combination with the quick pick numbers when the pool's tickets are purchased.

Just as a bit of encouragement for your group, let me tell you about a group of 10 co-workers in New Jersey who formed a pool a few years ago and have each been playing $2 a week since then. Last May, they won the New Jersey Pick-6 jackpot for $2.1 million. Each pool member will receive an after-tax amount of $8,760 a year for the next 20 years. The group plans to continue playing each week and says it is looking forward to their next win.

Why do some players keep track of winning and losing numbers?

Q: I don't understand what there is to be gained by keeping track of winning and losing lottery numbers. Why do some lottery players keep such close tabs on these numbers?

A: Some lottery players believe that there is a certain inevitability to the numbers that are drawn in lotteries, so they keep track of winning and losing numbers so that they can determine which numbers to play each week. Here are the theories.

Theory one: If the number has been drawn frequently in the past (a "hot" number), it has established a pattern of being drawn and is likely to keep being drawn in the future. A subscriber to this theory always plays the most frequently drawn numbers over the past months, hoping that those numbers will keep coming up and make him or her a winner.

Theory two: If the number hasn't been drawn often or lately (a "cold" number), it's time for it to come up in a drawing. Followers of this theory declare that the probability of these less frequently selected numbers hitting is very high. In essence, since the laws of inevitability and random selection declare that all numbers will be drawn sometime, it is likely that it is their turn to be selected soon. As time passes, the six least frequently drawn numbers are the numbers that are thought to be "inevitable" and they are played each week.

Theory three: Play it safe; pick three and three. Proponents of this theory say both theories one and two are correct, so a reasonable player will select the top three most winning numbers as well as the three numbers hitting least frequently. This combination covers all bases, they believe.

What do I think? I think random selection of numbers is always the best way to go.

I know what hot and cold numbers are, but what are good and bad numbers—and how do you win using them?

Q: What is the "good" numbers theory of lotto number selection? I've heard it mentioned twice in the past week. What is a "good" number? And are there "bad" numbers?

A: This "system" is also called the "Saintly System." It is a variation on using family and friends' birthdates as your numbers for playing lotto. The idea is that instead of just using birthdates of different people, some perhaps whom you don't even like, and others who are not very nice people, you should use only the birthdates of "good" people you really like.

According to this theory, if there is any justice in the universe, you stand a better chance of winning if you use the birthdates of truly good people whom you consider "saints," rather than the birthdates of ordinary people. This system is supposed to have special power if you also promise to reward your "saints" when you win.

My computer says "hot" numbers systems don't work!

Q: I have been impressed with your comments about lottery games, particularly when you say "playing the lottery is playing games of randomness." I have played lotto a few times, but never had high expectations because I was fully aware of the odds. But being a kind of amateur statistician and a computer "bug," I did tinker with a few computer programs. I thought you might be interested in what I discovered.

It didn't take long to figure out that looking for "trends" in winning numbers was about as worthwhile as expecting the second flip of a coin to be related to the first flip. So, using a spreadsheet, I decided to prove this to myself. I kept a record of all the Florida Lotto drawings starting with the first one on May 7, 1988, and determined what the most frequently winning numbers were, and also what I would have won if I had played these "hot" numbers for every one of the past 308 drawings through April 2, 1994.

The six most winning numbers were the following: 34 (drawn 51 times), 19 (drawn 49 times), 27 (drawn 49 times), 47 (drawn 49 times), 15 (drawn 48 times), 28 (drawn 47 times). Would I have won if I had played these same six numbers for each of the 308 drawings? Yes, but hardly anything to brag about. Six times I would have won with three numbers and two times with four numbers. So much for the "hot" numbers theory.

A: Thanks for the information. Your objective, statistical experience will be ignored by people who believe in "hot" number trends as the way to win the lottery. Why will they ignore your information? Because they want to believe that there is some plan, some higher power at work behind the scenes, determining which numbers are selected each drawing.

What is the number picking system that involves cutting up lottery tickets?

Q: A Texas Lottery winner supposedly has a unique system for picking his winning numbers that somehow involves cutting up lottery tickets. Do you know anything about this winning system?

A: Vidor, Texas, resident Oliver Dooley liked to play the lottery because he said it was fun. Last December, Dooley decided to try a new "secret" number picking method. He took all of his non-winning tickets, cut the numbers out and put them in a coffee cup. Then he pulled the little pieces of paper out one at a time, writing the numbers down. He then headed off to his lottery ticket retailer, bought his tickets and won $6.4 million with his "system."

"I made it fun," Dooley said, as he collected the first of 20 annual checks he will receive for $319,500.

What is the "mistake" theory of winning the lottery?

Q: I enjoy reading about all those lottery winners who have won the lottery because of some mistake. Your theory that the best way to win the lottery is to win by mistake is particularly fun. Have you heard of any new mistakes that have resulted in lottery wins?

A: It happens all the time. Ramon Gonzales had all six winning numbers for an Illinois Lotto drawing and won $4.9 million. But he won because of a mistake he made.

Gonzales used his wife's age, 29 (he thought), as one of the numbers he picked. In reality, Mrs. Gonzales is 28. If Ramon hadn't made this mistake, he would have had only 5 of 6 numbers and would have won only $2,342 instead of nearly $5 million.

And then there is Michael Graback of Basking Ridge, New Jersey, who normally buys four tickets for each drawing, but this time the clerk at the deli where he made his purchase punched out five tickets instead of four. Michael bought the fifth ticket also. Naturally, it was the last ticket, selected for him by mistake, which made Graback a multimillionaire. He won $16.8 million.

These are both good examples of my "Mistake Theory" of winning number selection. The best way to win a lotto jackpot is to hang around a lottery ticket seller and buy up any mistakes when tickets are printed. If you do this, you're bound to be a winner soon.

What numbers should I select if I don't want to share my winnings?

Q: If I want to have the best chance of not sharing the lotto jackpot with other people, and I don't want to use the lottery computer's quick-pick system, what numbers should I select?

A: I think that computer-generated random selection is still probably the best way to pick your lottery numbers (as long as the numbers selected randomly include a number or two above 30), but if you don't want to do that then I think you should select any set of numbers you want—as long as they are over 30. Why? It seems that the two most popular methods players use for selecting numbers for playing the lottery are to use calendar dates, such as birthdays and anniversaries, and making patterns on the bet slip.

Generally, these methods eliminate numbers above 31. Combinations such as 1-12-15-23-29-31 or 1-5-10-15-20-25 are guaranteed to have many winners if those numbers are drawn because so many players will have chosen to use the dates of the month and the months of the year. On the other hand, it is rare for a combination with numbers above 31 to even have one winner when it is drawn, let alone more than one winner, because these numbers are not dates.

How can I win more frequently playing instant games?

Q: I enjoy playing all of our state's instant games because I like the variety in the games and the excitement of scratching off the latex covering on the ticket and finding out immediately if I have won anything. Do you have any recommendations for someone like me that might help me win more frequently than

I do now? The excitement of playing is one thing, but I would like to have more of the excitement of winning.

A: There are two things you should do. Since all instant games are not created equal and with the same chances of winning, the first thing you should do is find out which of the several instant games available offers the best chances of winning and then only play that game, not all the instant games offered. For example, if three instant games are currently being offered, one game may have overall odds of winning of 1:3.75, another may have odds of 1:4.25, and the third may have odds of 1:5.54. You stand a much better chance of winning something if you play the game that offers chances of 1 in 3 rather than playing the games that offer chances of 1 in 4 or 1 in 5. Your ticket retailer has this information posted somewhere in his store. Just ask for it.

The second thing you can do is play the instant games that have more than one chance of winning something on the same ticket. When scratch-off games first were offered, they had only one play area to scratch off. You either won or lost. Then lotteries started putting two play areas on the same ticket making it possible to win (or lose) two times on one ticket. This created twice the fun and excitement for players. Now it is not uncommon for instant tickets to have three play areas to scratch off on the same ticket, with each area offering separate prizes. Three times the suspense and excitement for the same $1.

One state lottery, Idaho, has even offered a scratch-off ticket that has four scratch-off areas and four chances to win on the same ticket; however, this instant game costs $2. The odds of winning something with this game are 1:3.97. Several state lotteries now offer Bingo, a $2 game that has four bingo cards on it to play. Players find this four-chance game very appealing.

Is there a system for choosing which instant game to buy?

Q: Have you heard of any winning system for deciding which instant game ticket to buy, especially when there are six or more scratch-off games to choose from?

A: Surprisingly, there really are "systems" for picking scratch-off tickets—although very few of them are winning systems.

Some people only buy the most recent instant game. When a new game comes on the market, that's the one that gets purchased. Other players buy one of each game, and still other players always buy the oldest game—the one that has been for sale the longest.

I like Mike Hoover's winning system for picking scratch-offs. Mike, a Kansas Lottery player, recently scratched off a winning $5,000 ticket. When asked what his winning system was, he said that he always looked at the row of ticket dispensers to see how many tickets are left in each game. He then chooses the dispenser that has the fewest tickets left. He is convinced that winning tickets are heavier and sink to the bottom of the roll. I guess that is as good a system as any—and don't forget, Mike is $5,000 richer for employing it.

What winning number picking system uses cards?

Q: What was the "mysterious" number picking system that the man from Kansas used in October 1993 to win the $12 million Powerball jackpot. Someone said he "saw them in his cards." What does that mean?

A: Randall Frye, 38, of Wichita, Kansas, won $12,251,580 in the October 23, 1993, Powerball game. Frye's "mysterious" number picking system was really very simple. He had been playing the same numbers every week for six months and had picked them the first time by random selection with a deck of cards—you know, by drawing six cards out of a deck. Not too mysterious.

I've said it many times before: it doesn't matter which numbers you pick or how you pick them. Any set of numbers has the same chance of being drawn as every other set of numbers.

Should I buy several lotto tickets with the same number combinations?

Q: I usually only buy one lotto ticket each week and play the same set of numbers each time. Occasionally I will buy two or three extra tickets for a roll-over drawing but will play the same set of numbers on all the tickets. They are very special numbers that I know will win someday. My husband says that I am crazy and that I should play different sets of numbers when I buy extra tickets. He says that I should ask you about it. What do you think?

A: It probably will surprise your husband, but I am going to agree with you only because you are so confident of winning someday with your special numbers. Here's why.

Playing different sets of numbers always increases your chances of winning. For example, if you play a 6/49 game your chances of winning with one set of numbers are 1 in 14 million. If you play two different sets of numbers, your chances of winning with one of those sets is 1 in 7 million. For three different sets of numbers the chances become 1 in 4.6 million, and for four sets of numbers the chances are 1 in 3.5 million. You see? For each additional set of numbers you play, your chances of winning become better.

But, if you really do believe that your special numbers are the ones that will win for you and not the extra sets of numbers, go ahead and play those same numbers on each additional ticket you purchase. There is a major benefit of this if—or perhaps I should say when—you win. The amount you win will be greater and you will have to share less with other winners.

It works like this. Since each lotto jackpot is parimutuel, which means that each winning ticket gets an equal share of the jackpot, you will receive more than other winners if you have additional winning tickets. For example, let's imagine that you and two other people win a $10 million jackpot. If you each have one ticket, you each will receive $3.3 million. But if you have three tickets each with the winning numbers, and the other two winners each have one winning ticket, that means that there are five winning tickets. Each ticket is now worth $2 million. You will receive three-fifths of the $10 million jackpot, or $6 million. In this case, it definitely pays to have more tickets with the same set of numbers.

For example, take the case of Steven Vachon, who bought 40 tickets at a supermarket for a $1 million New Hampshire Lotto drawing. There were three winning tickets sold and fortunately Vachon had all three. Three of his tickets had the same winning numbers on them, simply in different order on each of the three tickets. He was unaware that the order in which the numbers are picked makes no difference. As a result, the winning numbers, 6-7-15-18-21-22, in different order, showed up on three of his tickets. He won the entire $1 million jackpot.

What would I do? Since I don't have any confidence in the inevitability of a special set of numbers being selected, I'd play different sets of numbers and go for the better odds.

Should I play different lottery games or just lotto?

Q: Our state lottery keeps coming up with "specials," promotional offers designed to get us to play the different lottery games. Up until now I've stuck to playing lotto, putting all my money each week into that game, but I am tempted at times to

spend some of that money on playing the other games even though you don't win large amounts. What do you think?

A: Play the other games also, especially if you are on a limited budget for tickets each week. Use part of your money to play lotto but also use part to play the other games where the chances of winning are much better than with lotto.

One of the few ways that you can increase your chances of winning is to play some of the low odds games such as the pick-3, -4, -5 and the instant scratch-off games. With these games your chances are very good that you will win occasionally, at least small amounts.

PART II

It's a Fact!

It's hard to believe, but U.S. lotteries are now creating millionaires at the rate of five new millionaires a day!

Am I more likely to win if I pick the numbers or if the lottery computer picks my numbers?

Q: Am I more likely to win the lottery by using numbers I pick or using numbers picked for me by the lottery quick-pick computer where I buy my lotto tickets?

A: Any set of numbers picked any old way has the same chance of winning as any other set of numbers. It doesn't matter how you pick your numbers, but what does matter is that you be lucky. In the nation's largest jackpot so far, the $118.8 million California jackpot, there were 10 tickets containing the winning numbers. According to lottery officials, five of those tickets were quick picks and five were selected by players.

Who gets the interest on lottery-invested winnings?

Q: When the lottery jackpot is won by someone and the winner is paid over a period of 20 years, I'm assuming that the total jackpot amount is put in an interest bearing bank account for the 20 years. My question is, who gets the interest on that money, the winner or the lottery?

A: The winner. What you may not understand, however, is that only half of the publicized jackpot amount is really available when it is won. It works like this.

Let's say the publicized weekly lotto grand prize is $1 million. In reality, the lottery only has half that amount, $500,000, in cash available for the winner, so what the lottery does is take that $500,000 and buys a $1 million annuity from a giant insurance company or bank. This annuity is really just a paid up savings account that promises to collect interest on the money (the $500,000) so that the interest and principle will total $1 million in 20 years. The annuity then pays a specified amount of money (one twentieth of $1 million) back to the annuity owner (the lottery winner) every year for 20 years.

By doing it this way, and by using the interest that is paid each year on the unpaid lottery winnings, state lotteries are able to offer jackpots that are twice as large as the actual amount of money available.

How many new millionaires have state lotteries created?

Q: How many new millionaires have state lotteries created since states started awarding million-dollar jackpots?

A: On October 8, 1970, in New York, the first person to be awarded $1 million received it in a special drawing. As is the case today in most lottery states, the winner was paid in 20 annual installments. Since that day, more than 6500 millionaires have been created.

New York, not surprisingly because of its years of awarding jackpots, is the leader in creating instant millionaires with over 700. Pennsylvania is second and Illinois is third. States like Florida and Texas create millionaires each week (Florida created over 60 last year) because of the large jackpots, but Florida and Texas have been at it for only a few years.

Millionaires are being created much faster now than just a few years ago because the games are now computerized. In the '70s, since the games were not computerized, states like New York were forced to cut off ticket sales hours or, in some cases, days early in order for all bets to be recorded and put onto microfilm.

Now, with on-line systems completely computerized, players are able to purchase tickets up to a few minutes before each drawing, thus encouraging larger jackpots, as well as guaranteeing weekly millionaires.

What is ironic is that many of the "millionaires" are that in name only. All but a relative few of these millionaires were paid in an annuity lasting anywhere from 10 to 26 years. Today, winners who win $1 million usually receive 20 annual payments of $50,000.

But before they get that money, 28% of the win is immediately deducted each year for federal taxes, leaving the winner with about $35,000. Sometimes state taxes are also deducted. Since a lottery win is considered earned income, the player usually pays additional taxes at the end of the year. This usually leaves a $1 million winner with about $30,000 a year and there aren't many people earning this amount who call themselves millionaires.

Is the IRS taxing lottery winnings more?

Q: Is it true that the IRS has increased the amount of taxes it takes out of lottery winnings before handing over the winnings? How much is the new tax?

A: The U.S. Congress passed a law in 1992 (H.R. 776), signed by President Bush, that increased the amount of federal income tax state lotteries must withhold beginning January 1, 1993. Lotteries must now withhold 28% from all prizes of more than $5,000. This is a 40% increase over the 20% that had been withheld prior to January 1, 1993.

This increase also includes all lotto payments made after January 1, 1993, even if the lotto prize was won before that date and annual payments are still continuing.

In addition, many states also have state taxes on lottery winnings ranging from 2% to 6%.

By the way, although the withholding rate was increased, your personal income tax rate is NOT increased by the new law.

What are the numbers that sometimes break the lottery bank?

Q: I understand that in the cash games such as pick-3 and pick-4 where a fixed prize amount is paid to winners, some days there are so many winners with the same numbers that the lottery pays out more than it takes in. Can you give me some idea of what those numbers are? I'm curious.

A: They are the same numbers in every state lottery. When they come up, the lottery officials know it will pay out more that day than it takes in because it knows there will be a lot of people playing those numbers.

The Virginia Lottery provides us with a good example. From 1991 to 1992, players broke the bank seven times, forcing the lottery to pay out much more than it took in. The numbers and dates are listed below.

4-4-1	7/06/91
1-2-3	9/24/91
9-9-9	11/07/91
7-7-7	1/21/92
3-3-3	1/31/92
1-2-3	3/04/92
4-1-1	4/03/92

As you can see from this list, numbers in a series and "lucky" numbers are played heavily in daily pick-3 games.

What are the record jackpots?

Q: Can you tell me how big the largest lottery jackpots have been and in what states they have been won?

A: The top 10 record jackpots are listed below, what states they were in, the dates they were won, and how many winning tickets shared the jackpot. In addition, I thought you might like to know what the highest individual prizes have been, who won them, when, in which states, and also what the largest jackpots were for 1993 and how many tickets shared the prize.

Record U.S. Jackpots

1. $118.8 million	CA	4/17/91	10 tickets
2. $115.57 million	PA	4/26/89	14 tickets
3. $111.2 million	WI	7/7/93	1 ticket
4. $106.5 million	FL	9/15/90	6 tickets
5. $90 million	NY	1/26/91	9 tickets
6. $89.78 million	FL	10/26/91	6 tickets
7. $89.5 million	DC	12/22/93	2 tickets
8. $86.0 million	FL	3/20/93	3 tickets
9. $69.94 million	IL	4/15/89	4 tickets
10. $68.56 million	CA	2/21/90	4 tickets

Highest Individual Prizes

1. Leslie Robins	$111.2 million	WI	7/7/93
2. Sheelah Ryan	$55.1 million	FL	9/3/88
3. Richard Hovis	$50 million	OH	10/10/90
4. Wommer & Despot	$46 million	PA	10/15/86
5. Thomas Tehee	$45.3 million	CA	12/5/90
6. Bill Madigan	$42 million	IL	8/26/89
7. Edwin Sherwin	$42 million	IL	5/19/90
8. Mike Wittkowski	$40 million	IL	9/1/84
9. John Evancho	$39.6 million	IL	12/24/88
10. James Soper	$39 million	IL	11/5/88

Top 10 U.S. Jackpots of 1993

1. $111.2 million	WI	07/07/93	1 ticket
2. $89.5 million	DC	12/22/93	2 tickets
3. $86 million	FL	3/20/93	3 tickets
4. $62.2 million	CA	3/10/93	3 tickets
5. $59.1 million	IN, MO	3/3/93	2 tickets
6. $52 million	PA	9/28/93	1 ticket

7.	$48.9 million	TX	7/7/93	3 tickets
8.	$48.6 million	TX	5/1/93	14 tickets
9.	$40 million	OH	6/16/93	1 ticket
	($26 million cap for one winner)			
10.	$38.6 million	TX	9/9/93	1 ticket

As you can tell from these lists, relatively few lottery states have huge lotto jackpots. The majority of lottery states routinely award grand prizes that are less than $3 million. The American public has gotten so used to $2-, $3-, and $4-million wins that those wins usually receive little publicity. It is only when roll-overs create jackpots of more than $20 million that the media makes the lottery and its winners a front page story.

How much money is spent playing lotteries worldwide?

Q: Do you have any idea how much money is spent playing lotteries worldwide? It must be an enormous amount.

A: It is enormous, over $70 billion in 1993.

If you were to rank countries with lotteries by total 1993 lottery sales, the United States would lead with over $25 billion, followed by Spain and Germany, each with over $6 billion, Japan with $4 billion and Canada with over $3 billion.

Who plays the lottery?

Q: Have lottery players changed in the past few years since lotteries have come to be accepted as providing a major part of many states' income bases? Has all of the media advertising for

lotteries made any difference in who plays? Are players older, richer, whiter now than 10 years ago, or have players stayed about the same over the years?

A: Surprisingly, things have stayed about the same over the years. Every state lottery conducts frequent surveys of its players to determine the answers to the questions that you raise. Although there is some difference in player profile from state to state, it is possible to combine those profiles to come up with an unscientific but fairly accurate picture of the average American lottery player in any state.

Of all adults (those 18 or over) in any lottery state, over 70% have played the lottery in the past year and at least 40% of all adults have played in the last two weeks. Most players are white (about 80%) and well educated. Eighty-five percent of players have at least a high school diploma and over 35% have attended college for one or more years. Younger people (under 30) don't play as frequently as older people (over 30). The largest group of players are the 35 to 44-year-olds (about 25% of all players). There are more men than women lottery players (about 56% to 44%), and very few players (under 20%) are in the low income category (below $15,000). About 80% of all players earn over $15,000, with 22% of current lottery players having an income of $35,000-$50,000. Twenty-three percent have annual incomes of over $50,000.

Surprised at this profile? Most people are. It is not the "poor, uneducated minorities" who are the "victims" of lotteries, as was charged 20 years ago when national debates raged about the morality of starting state lotteries.

What are the most commonly played lotto numbers?

Q: What are the most commonly played lotto number combinations? I know that if those numbers ever win, there will be so many winners that each person's share may only be a few dollars. I just want to make certain that I play different numbers.

A: The most commonly played lotto number combinations in most lottery states are

1. 01 02 03 04 05 06
2. 07 14 21 28 35 42
3. 05 10 15 20 25 30

In some of the high population lottery states (California, Florida, New York, Michigan, Illinois) you may have 50,000 people playing each of these sets of numbers. If one of those number combinations should happen to win a jackpot of $5 million, with 50,000 winners, each winner would receive after taxes about $70. The good news is that the lottery would pay each winner in one lump sum and not spread payments out over 20 years.

Which states give lotto winners a lump sum payment?

Q: Which states give lotto players a lump sum payment of the jackpot when they win?

A: Four states now offer lotto winners the jackpot in one lump sum: Arizona, Oregon, Indiana, and Ohio. Several other lottery states are considering giving their lotto players the option of either taking the money in one lump sum payment or of having the prize paid over several years. In states where a choice is now given, players must mark the appropriate box (cash option or annuity option) on the selection slip when they purchase their ticket. If the lump sum option is selected, winners receive half of the advertised jackpot amount in cash. If they select the annuity option, then the total advertised jackpot amount is paid over 20-25 years.

What are the mailing addresses of the state lotteries?

Q: What are the mailing addresses for the different state lotteries?

A: Frequently there are several mailing addresses for each state lottery, one address to send in ENTRY tickets, another address for lottery advertising, and perhaps another address for the central offices of the lottery. The addresses below are for the "main" office for each state lottery, the place where lottery officials hang out and conduct business.

Arizona State Lottery
4740 East University Drive
Phoenix, AZ 85034

California State Lottery
600 North Tenth Street
Sacramento, CA 95814

Colorado State Lottery
720 South Colorado
   Boulevard, Suite 110
Denver, CO 80222

Connecticut Lottery
P.O. Box 11424
Newington, CT 06111

Delaware State Lottery
Blue Hen Mall, Suite 202
Dover, DE 19901

District of Columbia Lottery
2102 Martin Luther King Jr.
   Avenue, SE
Washington, DC 20020

Florida State Lottery
Capitol Complex
250 Mariott Drive
Tallahassee, FL 32399

Georgia State Lottery
250 Williams Street, Suite 3000
Atlanta, GA 30303

Hoosier Lottery
Pan Am Plaza
201 South Capitol Avenue,
    Suite 1100
Indianapolis, IN 46225

Idaho Lottery
1199 Shoreline Lane,
    Suite 100
Boise, ID 83707

Illinois Lottery
676 North St. Clair
Chicago, IL 60611

Indiana State Lottery
201 South Capital Avenue,
    Suite 1100
Indianapolis, IN 46255

Iowa Lottery
2015 Grand Avenue
Des Moines, IA 50312

Kansas Lottery
128 North Kansas Avenue
Topeka, KS 66603

Kentucky Lottery
Two Paragon Center, Suite 400
6040 Dutchmans Lane
Louisville, KY 40205

Louisiana Lottery
11200 Industriplex Boulevard
    Suite 150-190
Baton Rouge, LA 70809

Maine State Lottery
219 Capitol Street—State House,
    Suite 30
Augusta, ME 04332

Maryland Lottery
Plaza Office Center, Suite 204
6776 Reisters Town Road
Baltimore, MD 21215

Massachusetts State Lottery
Office of the State Treasurer
Statehouse Room 227
Boston, MA 02133

Michigan Lottery
101 East Hillsdale
Lansing, MI 48909

Minnesota State Lottery
2645 Long Lake Road
Roseville, MN 55113

Missouri Lottery
1823 Southridge Drive
Jefferson City, MO 65102

Montana Lottery
2525 North Montana Avenue
Helena, MT 59601

Multi-State Lottery Association
(Powerball)
1200 35th Street, Suite 701
West Des Moines, IA 50165

Nebraska Lottery
301 Centennial Mall South
Lincoln, NE 68509

New Hampshire State Lottery
75 Fort Eddy Road
Concord, NH 03301

New York Lottery
One Broadway Center
Schenectady, NY 12301

New Jersey Lottery
CN 041
Trenton, NJ 08625

Ohio Lottery
615 Superior Avenue NW
Cleveland, OH 44113

Oregon State Lottery
P.O. Box 12649
Salem, OR 97308

Pennsylvania Lottery
Department of Revenue
2850 Turnpike Industrial Drive
Middletown, PA 17057

Rhode Island Lottery
1425 Pontiac Avenue
Cranston, RI 02920

South Dakota Lottery
207 East Capitol, Suite 200
Pierre, SD 57501

Texas Lottery
P.O. Box 16630
Austin, TX 78761

Tri-State Megabucks
73 Winthrop Street
Statehouse Station #30
Augusta, ME 04333

Vermont Lottery
P.O. Box 420
South Barre, VT 05670

Virginia State Lottery
P.O. Box 4689
Richmond, VA 23220

State of Washington Lottery
814 Fourth Avenue
Olympia, WA 98506

West Virginia Lottery
312 MacCorkle Avenue SE
Charleston, WV 25327

Wisconsin Lottery
P.O. Box 8941
Madison, WI 53708

How much lottery prize money goes unclaimed?

Q: I neglected to turn in a winning instant game ticket until it was too late and lost $5 as a result. Do you have any idea how much lottery money goes unclaimed because players fail to claim their winnings before the time they have to collect them runs out?

A: Lots and lots. For example, just in the state of California during 1990, more than $32.6 million in winning lotto and scratch-off prizes were never claimed. Over $30 million of that was for unclaimed lotto prizes, and $2 million was from scratch-offs. Ninety percent of all this unclaimed money was for lower-tier winnings in the $5 range.

People frequently lose winning tickets, forget about them until it is too late to collect, or send winning tickets in to lottery offices for payment without having the correct lottery address and the tickets get lost or destroyed.

What happens to uncollected prize money?

Q: What happens to lottery prize money that doesn't get collected by the winners? It's already been set aside for the winners, so it must go somewhere if it is not claimed.

A: Surprisingly, there is a large amount of money that is unclaimed from all state lottery games. Occasionally the lotto grand prize in some states is not collected, but frequently smaller prizes in other pick-3, pick-4, pick-5 games, and even in scratch-off games are not claimed. New York state, for example, has had more than $100 million in unclaimed winnings since it started its lottery games.

In New York, as is the case in many states, those unclaimed winnings go back into the state treasury after the prize deadlines have expired. Other states such as Florida, Illinois and California return their unclaimed winnings to the prize pool and it is paid out to other winners in other weeks. Unclaimed winnings never get lost.

Are collectors buying used lottery tickets?

Q: Do you have any idea what the value might be to a collector of our state's first instant game lottery ticket? For no good reason I saved the first scratch-off ticket I bought rather than throw it away when I found out it wasn't a winner. Lottery ticket collecting is getting to be a big deal, like stamps or baseball cards, and some of the early state lottery tickets are valuable. What can you tell me about this?

A: Lottery ticket collecting is getting to be a popular hobby across the country. You are not the only person who "for no good reason" saves scratched-off instant game tickets. The Lottery Collector's Society was formed several years ago to unite interested collectors across the country. Since then the LCS has added hundreds of members, produces lottery ticket catalogs, trades between members, and holds an annual convention.

In June this year, the annual convention of the Society was held in Port Huron, Michigan (which just happens to be the town in which I grew up). Collectors came from all over the country to buy, sell and trade tickets. One collector sold an Illinois lottery ticket for $1800 and turned down an offer of $50,000 for his entire collection. Another collector turned down $500 for an early Michigan ticket. There was even a canceled $250,000 winner from Michigan's Bicentennial Commemorative series and a lottery pin from the former Soviet Union featuring the sickle and hammer inside a red star. One collector from Wisconsin has collected tickets from 199 countries and proudly displays a ticket from the last lottery in Cuba 35 years ago next to lottery tickets from such places as Saudi Arabia, Sri Lanka, Austria and Germany. One collector from Los Angeles spent $500 buying used California lottery tickets to complete his California collection.

Active collectors say there is money to be made in lottery tickets in the future and that we would be smart if we traded our used lottery tickets with people in other states for their state's tickets. So how much is your Florida ticket worth? You would probably find out if you joined The Lottery Collector's Society, 1007 Lutrell Street, Knoxville, TN 37917.

And one more thing. You might think about collecting *unscratched* lottery tickets like I do. It is difficult to not scratch off a ticket when you purchase it, but think about it. In the years to come, having an old lottery ticket that is unscratched will be like having an uncirculated rare coin.

If everyone in the world shared equally the lottery prize money awarded so far, how much would each person have?

Q: Here's a good question for you: If all the prize money won in lotteries worldwide since lotteries began was divided up among the entire population of the world, how much would each person alive today receive?

A: I am certain that given enough time and an advanced degree in math, I could give you a very good answer—and maybe even a correct one. But I don't have the time or the degree so I will have to give you an estimate.

The Maryland Lottery reports that it has given away over $5 billion in prizes since the lottery began in 1973. That is enough money to give everyone in the world a $1 dollar bill. But, keep in mind that states like California, New York, and Florida each give that amount to winners every two years. Plus, there are about 140 lotteries in the world, and some of them have been around for hundreds of years. That's a lot of prize money over the years.

So what's my educated guess? I'd say about $1,000 per person for everyone alive today.

When there is a giant $100 million jackpot won, are all possible number combinations usually played?

Q: Do you have any idea whether or not all the possible six-number combinations are played when a state has a $100 million jackpot? With those millions of players buying tickets, is it possible for it to roll over again?

A: It's not likely. Let me give you an example. In Florida's 6/49 lotto, there are 13,983,816 possible six-number combinations. By the time of the drawing for the Florida Lottery's $106 million jackpot on September 15, 1990, all but about 57,000 combinations had been played. That means that 99.6% of the possible combinations had been played. With 57,000 combinations still unplayed it was possible for it to roll over again—just not likely.

Where can I get a list of winning number combinations?

Q: Do you know where I could get a list of all winning number combinations in all the lottery games in the United States since state lotteries began in the early '60s? Or doesn't such a list exist?

A: It exists. You will want to get a copy of Ron Shelley's *Lottery Numbers Book*, published by Intergalactic Publishing Company. Your local bookstore can order it for you. Price? Around $28.00.

Which lottery game has the most sales?

Q: Which lottery game generates the most sales: lotto, the daily pick-3, -4, or -5 games, or the instant games?

A: It depends on the state. In the high population states like New York, Florida, and California, lotto is the leader. Surprisingly to most people who believe that lotto always accounts for the most ticket sales in every state, in smaller population states, scratch-off games produce most of the income. For example, in the 1992-93 fiscal year, the state of Minnesota, a medium-sized state, offered several lottery games: Powerball, which is a lotto-like game; Daily 3, a pick-3 game; Gopher 5, a twice-a-week pick-5 game; and 14 new scratch-off games. Lottery players spent a total of $328.8 million on lottery tickets, with 68% of that money being spent on scratch-off games. Powerball accounted for only 21% of sales.

Do lotteries really have any impact on a state's economy?

Q: Are state lotteries really having any impact on states' economies? Isn't the money that players are spending really just money they would spend anyway, but for different things?

A: You are correct. Lottery purchases by residents of lottery states aren't significantly impacting the states' economies;

money is just being circulated differently. But there is an impact—very significant for some lottery states—that comes from
establishing new lottery-related businesses necessary for running a lottery and also from lottery purchases by out-of-state
players. This impact takes the form of direct and indirect benefits of that new money. When a lottery is introduced into a
state, the state draws in money that would not have been there
otherwise. That money creates new income and new jobs. Each
state lottery creates thousands of new jobs when it starts up, including lottery supplier jobs as well as positions for full-time
lottery employees. Nationally, hundreds of thousands of lottery-related jobs have come into existence with the creation of
37 state lotteries. A good example of this is the state of Oregon.
The Oregon Lottery recently announced that 22,000 new jobs
have been created throughout the state because of the Oregon
Lottery.

Even in the small population states, many new jobs have
been created. The South Dakota Lottery decided in 1989 to
add video lottery to its other lottery games. In just one year,
from September 1989 to September 1990, more than 2,000
new video lottery-related jobs alone were created statewide.
Those 2000 jobs are in addition to the other lottery-related jobs
that were created.

In some lottery states, like Michigan for example, and not
counting lottery employees or retail clerks hired to sell lottery
tickets, nearly 200 Michigan residents have been employed by
the companies that produce the lottery's instant games and on-
line tickets. In addition, these companies—G TECH and Webcraft—do business with other Michigan firms. G TECH calcu-
lates it will purchase in excess of $125 million in products,
goods and services during the 10-year lifespan of their contract
with Michigan. Webcraft, the printer of Michigan Lottery instant tickets, estimates it purchased more than $2 million worth
of goods and services in the state last year. The Michigan Lottery itself also spent about $13 million with Michigan printing
companies, advertising and public relations firms, newspapers
and radio stations to produce advertising, point-of-sale promotional pieces and media buys.

In states like Florida, New York, or California, where visitors from out-of-state are a major industry already, it is easy to see the possibility of an influx of new money caused by visitors also playing the state lottery. The same thing also happens to a lesser extent in smaller lottery states with fewer visitors. Louisiana is a good example.

Dr. Loren Scott and Dr. James Richardson, professors of economics at Louisiana State University, conducted a study called "The Economic Impact of the Louisiana Lottery" in 1993. They concluded that in addition to the substantial amount of money spent by Louisiana residents on the lottery, the Louisiana Lottery brought $14.6 million in new money into the state economy from out-of-state visitors. The multiplier effect of that new money by itself brought a $28 million increase in additional Louisiana business sales, provided new household earnings of about $9.2 million for Louisianians, and created 545 new jobs for residents. The study noted that had the state legislature been forced to raise the money by taxing money that the Louisiana Lottery transferred to the treasury, it would have required increasing the general sales tax by about one-half of a percentage point or raising the tax on food and drugs by about 1.5 percentage points.

Has anyone won prizes in all lotto prize categories?

Q: Do you know of any lotto player who has won in all lotto prize categories? I have won prizes for matching 3-of-6, 4-of-6, 5-of-6, and am hoping that one of these days I will win that elusive 6-of-6 jackpot.

A: I know of only one player who has won in all lotto prize categories in his state's lotto. Pasquale Benenati, 59, became the first California Lottery player in 1991 to win every prize category while playing the old 6/53 lotto game. In March 1989, Benenati won a $5.18 million jackpot. Since then he's won prizes for a 3-of-6 win, a 4-of-6 win, a 5-of-6 win, and even the 5-of-6 plus bonus number win last November which was worth $150,612. What was his number picking system? He let the computer randomly generate his numbers.

What is the largest pool to win a lotto jackpot?

Q: What is the largest lottery pool to win a lotto jackpot?

A: The "Lucky 372," a 372-member group composed of members of the Fifth Ward Athletic Association, a private, non-profit, all-male organization founded in 1933, won $8.6 million in the July 15, 1991, New Jersey Pick-6 Lotto. The first of the pool's 20 annual installments of $308,816 amounted to $830 for each member.

Was the Catholic church responsible for creating the first lottery?

Q: A friend told me that the Catholic Church invented and conducted the first lottery sometime in the 16th century. Could that be true? I know that the Catholic Church sponsors fund-raising games of chance such as bingo, but do we also owe the invention of lotto to the Church?

A: Your friend's information is a bit tangled up. As far as any-one knows, the Dutch conducted the first public lottery on record in 1434 in an effort to raise money for the town of Sluis. Many European cities followed suit and used lotteries to raise money for city and community projects.

Nearly 80 years after the Dutch started the lottery business, the game we know today as lotto was born in Rome, but it wasn't invented or conducted by the Catholic Church, although the Church was indirectly involved. It was time to pick a new Pope, and there was much speculation among the citizens of Rome concerning which 12 of the 99 cardinals eligible to become Pope would be the finalists. Some enterprising person got the idea that it would be fun—and profitable—to conduct a contest guessing which 12 of the 99 possible choices would become the finalist. In essence, the game they were playing was a 12/99 lotto game, and consequently lotto as we know it was born.

Since then, lotteries have been started in over 130 countries. In the U.S., with the recent addition of Texas as a lottery state, 36 states plus the District of Columbia now conduct lotteries, with the likelihood that all 50 states will be conducting lotteries by the end of this decade.

In which state do people spend the most money per person on lottery tickets?

Q: I'm having an argument with some fellow lottery players about how much people spend on lottery tickets each week. On a per capita basis, in which state do people spend the most on lottery tickets? I'd bet it's California, New York and Florida in that order.

A: I hope you didn't bet any money on this because you lose. California and New York aren't even in the top 10, and Florida is number seven. Surprisingly, players in Massachusetts are clearly number one. They are way ahead of players in other states—by nearly 50%—when it comes to weekly lottery ticket purchasing. For the 36 operating lotteries in the United States, the top 10 rankings in per capita lottery sales each week are:

1. Massachusetts	$6.13
2. District of Columbia	$4.66
3. South Dakota	$4.26
4. Maryland	$3.40
5. New Jersey	$3.37
6. Connecticut	$3.36
7. Florida	$3.28
8. Ohio	$3.17
9. Virginia	$2.75
10. Illinois	$2.66

How long has lotto been around?

Q: How long have state lotteries been running lotto? I have been playing state lottery games for years, but it seems that until recently all I ever was able to play were scratch-off games. Now, the different lotto games seem to have become the important games.

A: I know it is hard to believe, but the first lotto game was pioneered by the New York Lottery in the U.S. in 1978. Prior to then, instant games were the only thing available. All it took, however, was for one Brooklyn maintenance man to win a $5 million jackpot, and the resulting coast-to-coast coverage resulted in the effort to get a lotto game going in every lottery state as quickly as possible. Within the next three years, 12 more states started a lotto game.

So you see, it really hasn't been very long that we've been able to play lotto. Don't you wonder what form the next big lottery game will take?

What percentage of the U.S. population lives in lottery states?

Q: I know that we now have 37 lottery states (actually, 36 states and the District of Columbia), but I am wondering what percentage of the U.S. population lives in those 37 states, and are these generally the economically poor or rich states?

A: Seventy-four percent of our states now have a lottery, and about 80% of the population lives in those 37 lottery states. This population accounts for a little over 80% of U.S. personal income.

PART III

That's an Incredible Offer!

"Find Out Your Lucky Lottery Numbers. Call Now For Sensational Results With Rare Gifted Psychic Numerologists on the Live Psychic Advisor Network! Let Live Psychics help you understand the past and create the future you desire, including your Lucky Numbers. All it takes is a call. Let's Talk About YOU! Talk to a Live Psychic Now! 1-900-[555-5555]. $3.99 per minute."

[A magazine advertisement.]

Do some lottery pools guarantee winning?

Q: Is it true that some lottery pools guarantee that their members will win the lottery?

A: Yes, but keep reading.

You are probably referring to a few commercial lottery pools that have been heavily advertising recently for members and promising that pool members will win every time, at least something.

One such commercial pool, the Millionaire 200 Club, specializes in playing the Australian lottery and sets up multiple pools of 200 members each. Here's how it works.

When you join one of the pools, you'll join 199 others. Each person has an equal share. And because you play as a group, you will have many more chances to win than you could playing by yourself.

You choose the pool you wish to join depending on how much you want to spend. Each pool costs a different amount, with corresponding numbers of chances. The guarantee for each pool ranges from $1,000 to $8,000 depending on the amount you pay to join the pool.

For example, for $149 each, 200 people are put in a pool that purchases 15,120 chances to win the Australian lottery, and your pool is guaranteed to win a minimum of $4,000. If your pool doesn't win at least that amount, the sponsoring company pays the difference out of its pockets.

Remember, though, the $4,000 guarantee is not yours alone. You have to divide it with 199 other members of the pool. Your share of these "guaranteed winnings" is $20.

Also note that if 20 friends, co-workers or neighbors formed their own pool and each contributed the same $149, that pool could purchase 29,800 chances—nearly twice as many as the 15,120 promised by the commercial pool. And even if this local pool didn't win the jackpot, I suspect that a pretty good chunk of cash would be won by the pool just on tickets that correctly picked three, four or five winning numbers.

Be wary of these too-good-to-be-true lottery offers. They *are* too good to be true.

Was this "opportunity" really just another lottery scam?

Q: I think I was offered a chance to be tricked out of some money last week. A lady walked up to me on the street and asked if she could talk to me. She had a heavy accent, was a bit hard to understand, and proceeded to tell me that she had a problem. She said that she had just won $1,000 dollars with a scratch-off ticket but couldn't collect the money because she was in the country illegally. She said she was looking for someone who would cash in the ticket for her, and she would be glad to split the winnings with whoever cashed in the ticket. She showed me the ticket and sure enough it was a $1,000 winner. When I said that I would cash in the ticket for her, she said that I had to give her $500, her share, in advance because once I cashed in the ticket she had no guarantee that I would split the winnings with her. The problem was, I didn't have $500. Once I said that, the lady left real fast. Later, talking over the incident with my family, they pointed out all the ways that something could have gone wrong with that "opportunity." They think it was a trick of some kind, what do you think?

A: You are lucky you didn't have the $500 because you would have lost it. Your family was correct. You almost got caught in a common lottery scam that tricks hundreds of people out of their money every year. It works like this.

If you had given $500 to the lady and tried to cash in the ticket, one of two things might have happened: 1. The lottery ticket retailer would have told you that the ticket was invalid because the game was over and the deadline for cashing in tickets had passed, or 2. when the clerk checked the serial number on your "winning" ticket, he would have found out that the ticket had already been cashed in once and had later been stolen. At that point you might have been speaking to the police, trying to explain how you had possession of that ticket.

Not long ago, a Florida man committed suicide as a result of this scam. Distraught over losing his life savings in a similar lottery ticket swindle, he drove his car into a canal and fought off a man who tried to rescue him. Earlier, two con men had cheated the man out of $7,000 by saying they were illegal aliens and couldn't cash a winning lottery ticket that was later found to be worthless. They offered to split their winnings if the man would put up the $7,000 as "good faith money."

There is no rule against illegal immigrants, or anyone else, legal or illegal, cashing in winning tickets.

Which lottery winner is now selling magic lottery-winning candles?

Q: Have your heard anything about a lottery winner who is now selling magic candles that will help people win the lottery?

A: Unfortunately, I am aware of the lottery winner you are talking about. If you have read my other lottery writings, you also know my attitude toward people, lottery winners or not, who sell mystical, magical or religious objects that are supposed to help players win the lottery. To say that I disapprove would be an understatement.

Florida Lottery winner Lorraine Glick has begun advertising a $9.95 (plus $3 for shipping) "Magic Candle" for sale which the ads say Glick "will personally anoint with the MONEY OIL" that made her a millionaire. Glick won one third of a $13 million jackpot in August of 1989, after praying and then buying a "money candle" that she anointed with "money oil." Oh yes, she also bought five lotto tickets using random number selection.

Is there a chance of winning playing the Canadian Lottery by mail?

Q: My husband has sent money to a Canadian Lotto 6/49 Group Share Plan. I say it is a waste of money. He was sent a certificate showing 84 sets of 6 numbers being played for himself and his group in the near future. Have you heard of this program, and do you think he has a chance of winning anything? I told him I'd rather see him spend his money in our own state playing our own lottery games. At least he would know if the money is actually spent as intended. I am interested to hear your comments on this.

A: This is just one of the many companies soliciting U.S. players to play Canadian lotteries—and breaking the law in doing so. It is against U.S. postal regulations to use the U.S. mail to solicit people to play the lottery. Many companies do so regularly, making certain that nothing on the outside of the envelope indicates that it contains a lottery solicitation, since otherwise the mail would be confiscated before it reaches you.

What do I think? I think you are correct and your husband would be better off playing your own state's lottery games. He paid nearly three times what it would have cost him to play a lotto game with the same odds in his own state, and on top of that, he really doesn't know if his wagers were made. And practically speaking, how would he ever know if they weren't? What's more, there are no advantages (in spite of what the solicitation said) for U.S. citizens in playing Canadian lotteries. Canadian jackpots are smaller than U.S. jackpots, and those highly publicized "tax-free" winnings are tax-free only to Canadian citizens, not to U.S. citizens. U.S. citizens pay U.S. taxes on Canadian lottery winnings. It makes more sense to me for your husband to gather a few friends and family members and form his own pool to play state lottery games. He'll definitely get more for his money.

And one last thing: your husband also violated the law and U.S. postal regulations by sending money and order forms to buy his shares in the Canadian lottery pool. He's not likely to go to jail even if the authorities find out, but now that he knows it is against the law, encourage him not to break it again.

Can you win a $300 million jackpot in the Canadian Lottery?

Q: I'm tempted to play the Canadian lotto 6/49 game for one main reason. The advertising I receive for it says the jackpots are up to $300 million, and I like playing the big jackpot games. What do you think?

A: If that is your reason for playing the Canadian lotto 6/49, then you definitely should not be playing it. All that slick mail that you receive from Canadian companies trying to get you to play Canadian lotteries is very deceptive. It talks about "$300 million in prizes" but that is not one jackpot, that is the estimated total of jackpot prize money for a year's worth of drawings. Drawings are held twice a week, so that means that $300 million is spread between 104 drawings. Each drawing may offer a jackpot of about $3 million.

What are the largest jackpots that have been awarded so far in the Canadian lotto 6/49? The top five are listed below. Note that the largest is only $15 million, and these "big" jackpots don't happen very often.

1. $15.5 million, April 1, 1989
2. $13.8 million, January 14, 1984
3. $11.4 million, September 3, 1988
4. $11.2 million, January 12, 1985
5. $11.1 million, January 16, 1988

So where are all these giant multi-million-dollar jackpots you are supposed to be able to win in Canada? They don't exist.

If you want big jackpots, play Florida, California, New York, Illinois, Pennsylvania. These states routinely have jackpots that are $20 million or more. I've said it before. Stay away from any lottery "offer" you receive through the mail. You won't get what you think you're getting when you play those foreign lotteries.

Why was a Canadian lottery solicitation mailed from Panama?

Q: I'd be interested in your opinion of the enclosed material I got in the mail. It says it is a "Verification of Canadian lottery eligibility for two weeks." Evidently it is a solicitation to get me to play the Canadian lottery. What I don't understand is that no person or company is named and only a post office box number is given. It was apparently airmailed to me from Panama, of all places, but the money is to be sent to a box in Vancouver. Looks like a scam to me.

A: What you and hundreds of thousands of Americans have received is the latest monthly mailing from Canada's largest subscription company specializing in getting gullible Americans to play one of the lotteries offered in Canada. The company that is responsible for mailing you this illegal piece of mail— and it is illegal to send lottery materials or lottery solicitations through the U.S. mail—is CAN WIN, a Vancouver-based operation. You'll note that there is no indication on the outside of the envelope that it contains lottery materials. Consequently, postal authorities can't confiscate it, and they are not allowed to open it to find out what is in it.

Why was it postmarked and mailed from Panama? Simple. The postage rates from Panama to the U.S. are a lot cheaper than the rates from Canada to the U.S.

And what about the "offer" you received? It is a lousy offer. They invite you to "Pay only $9.95. The computer will pick 6 numbers for you and play them in 4 Canadian Lotto 6/49 drawings." Let's see, the offer is to give you four lotto tickets for

$9.95, plus 40¢ postage. Does that sound like any kind of bargain to you, especially when you can get ten tickets for $10—not just four—for a 6/49 lotto game here in the U.S. with much bigger weekly jackpots?

And don't be fooled by statements declaring that Canadian Lotto winnings are tax free. They are, but only for Canadians. When you bring lotto winnings into this country you pay U.S. taxes on them.

My advice? Stay away from all lottery solicitations you receive in the mail.

Is there a global lottery conspiracy?

Q: Have you heard anything about the "Office of Lottery Intelligence" located in Washington, DC, or its monthly publication? I just received some mail from that office inviting me to join the "World Intelligence Network" (WIN) for $15 a year and receive their monthly news report on the secret war raging in the world over lotteries and lotto-dollars. The letter I got says that this is a secret organization with 60,000 agents worldwide gathering information about lotteries and how the countries of the world are secretly maneuvering to capture the maximum share of world lotto-dollars. Apparently whoever controls the lotteries of the world also controls the politics of the world. Also, for that same $15 membership fee you are entered into a "major, world class lottery game" for the term of the membership. For 52 weeks, you are given a lottery ticket twice a week—that's 104 tickets! Sounds like a good deal to me. What do you think?

A: I think that the only intelligence in this "World Intelligence Network" is the intelligence people use when they throw this "offer" in the trash. This is just another attempt to get you to spend your money on a monthly newsletter—and one that appears to me to be full of fabricated lottery information and speculation rather than helpful and useful facts.

For example, here are some lottery opinions that the newsletter is pushing:

* When Bush and Gorbachev met in Helsinki a few years ago to discuss Iraq, they really discussed Russia's plans to announce a global lottery to raise lotto-dollars to bail out Russia's failing economy. But Bush laid down the law to Gorbachev and said no because America will not stand for any disruption of its own key lottery games.

* China is preparing to introduce its own global lottery and require that every one of its 1.1 billion people in China—plus the 500 million Chinese people spread throughout the world—buy a $1 lottery ticket every week. That's 1.6 billion dollars every week to benefit the People's Republic of China.

* 60,000 WIN agents worldwide (that's more than the KGB, British intelligence, French intelligence, Israeli intelligence, and CIA combined) are said to be gathering lottery information "at great risk to their personal safety."

Had enough?

And about that Washington, DC, "Office of Lottery Intelligence"—I checked and it doesn't exist except on the letterhead of the solicitation letter sent you asking for $15. If you do decide to join, you send your money to an address in Las Vegas. What does this tell you?

And that promise to enter you into a lottery twice a week for a year? If you read closely you will see that *one* set of numbers ("personally chosen by the Director of Intelligence") will be played. Not one set for each person who joins, *one* single set of numbers for everyone. It is a pool of all subscribers sharing one ticket with one number combination. You—and everyone else—will receive an equal share of the winnings if that one set of numbers wins anything.

Save your money. This is just another not-so-clever lottery related scam with a new global conspiracy twist to it.

Does Lotto-Clock really pick winning numbers?

Q: It just saw an advertisement in a magazine for a "Lotto-clock" that supposedly selects your lottery numbers for you. The ad said, "Not only does LOTTO-CLOCK give you winning lottery numbers, it also keeps accurate time." I don't really care about the accurate time, but I would like some help with picking winning numbers. Do you know anything about this clock? Does it work?

A: I've seen the ads for this lucky clock also, and have been tickled by the thought of a clock picking my lotto numbers. The cost is $39.95 (on sale for $29.95). Does it work? Well, it probably tells time, and it probably does pick random lottery numbers, but does it pick WINNING lottery numbers? Not any better or worse than you do.

The thing that you are forgetting is that no person or no thing can pick *winning* lottery numbers. All anyone or any of the scores of random number selection gadgets for sale can do is pick numbers that may possibly turn out to be winning numbers. The people who write the ads for these number picking gadgets work hard at implying in their advertisements that their gadget somehow is able to know and pick winning numbers, but that's not true. The best that you can hope for if you buy this clock is that some of the numbers it picks for you *may* be winning numbers, but you should be prepared for it to pick you thousands of losing numbers also.

And one more thing. If you want someone or something to pick your numbers for you, why pay for that service? The lottery does it for free with their computerized quick pick system where you buy your tickets.

Does psychic number selection offer hope?

Q: I don't really know whether or not I believe in things like numerology, astrology, Tarot card reading or psychic advisors, but I guess I am open to the possibility of foretelling the future. Although I have never consulted people in these areas, I am tempted to find out if they might be able to see some winning lottery numbers in my future. Recently I have been seeing television commercials directed at lottery players promoting a "Psychic Hot-Line" 900 number that you could call to have the psychic tell you the future winning lottery numbers. The commercials always feature people claiming to be lottery winners who have won three, four, five, even six times using the numbers the psychic has given them. I have even seen an advertisement for one of these psychic hotlines in our local newspaper. What do you think? Should I spend the money and see if the psychic can make me a winner?

A: Only if you have money to waste. If this is the case, then why not? It might be very interesting and enlightening for you.

I have also seen these commercials and advertisements for psychic hotlines aimed at lottery players. These hotlines seem to be the latest scam aimed at making money off of frustrated lottery players who keep hoping to win the lottery. I have a few observations about these businesses.

First, these psychic "services" are expensive. When you call the 900 numbers you are charged by the minute and every effort is made to keep you on the line for as many minutes as possible. This could be expensive advice.

Second, those "winners" in the commercials are misleading at the very least. If they really have won three, four, five, or six times, it has been only small prizes, not big jackpots, otherwise the names of these "winners" would have been made public and reported by the media. Winning lower-tier prizes is not so hard to do. Nearly every lottery player I know has won small prizes at least a few times, and without any psychic help.

Third, not even the people who are behind the psychic hotlines believe that their "psychics" can predict winning lottery numbers. If you'll look closely the next time you see one of these commercials or advertisements, you will see the following statement printed very small at the bottom of the television screen or at the bottom of the advertisement: "For entertainment purposes only." This disclaimer keeps the "psychic" from being sued when the predicted lottery numbers don't win. But really, think about it. If a psychic could actually predict winning lottery numbers, would that psychic be telling others what those winning numbers were? Not a chance. Why share the jackpots? The psychic would play those winning numbers in a few lotteries, win a hundred million dollars or so and retire from the psychic business, not wear out the telephone giving advice at $25-$35 a shot.

So, what do I think? I think that all of these different services that offer to select winning lottery numbers for players are scams preying on gullible people. There really ought to be a law against all of these number picking operations unless they simply say, "If you don't want to guess your own numbers, I'll guess them for you for a fee." At least a service that says this is making no claims of any sort that the numbers picked will be winners.

What can I do about a dishonest ticket seller?

Q: A few months ago, I bought a lottery scratch-off ticket at a gas station nearby. The ticket stated that if you matched two numbers you would win that amount. It also said that if you un-covered a dollar sign along with the two numbers you would win twice the amount of the matching numbers. When I scratched my tickets I found a dollar sign and two $40 amounts. I thought that I had won $80. When I gave it to the clerk I told him I wasn't familiar with this game but that I thought that I had won $80. He looked at the ticket but said that it was no good because the dollar sign wasn't lined up properly with the numbers. I accepted his explanation with some disappoint-ment. He kept the ticket.

About two weeks ago on a trip up north I purchased the same type of ticket at a 7-11 store. Upon scratching the covering off I found exactly the same arrangement of numbers and a dollar

sign that my other ticket had, except that this time it was $2 and $2 in place of the $40 and $40. I was about to discard it but my friend took it to the store clerk and the clerk gave her $4. My friend explained to the clerk what had happened earlier with the other ticket at the gas station and this clerk said that it sounded like the first clerk had ripped me off by keeping my ticket and cashing it in. Is there anything that I can do about this?

A: If you are asking me if there is any way for you to get your $80, the answer is no. But there is something you can do. You can register a complaint with the state lottery.

Every state lottery is plagued with a certain number of dishonest ticket sellers who are taking advantage of players like yourself, but each lottery is committed to locating them and getting rid of them. The first thing you should do is call your lottery's toll-free number (available on the back of tickets, posted in stores where lottery tickets are sold, or available from information) so that you can speak to someone and register your complaint. The lottery will in turn tell the owner of the gas station that a complaint has been registered against one of his/her employees. Ticket retailers are very sensitive about this because if too many complaints are registered, the seller could lose the right to sell lottery tickets.

The next time you are unsure about a ticket or the information a ticket seller gives you, hang on to your ticket and take it to another ticket seller and see if you get the same answer.

Why would a lottery book have two selling prices?

Q: Why would a book on lotto wheeling systems be offered for sale by mail for two different prices, $49.95 or $39.95? You get the book for the lower price if you agree to inform the publisher of any lottery wins. You pay the higher price if you decide to keep any winnings secret. What's really going on here?

A: Clever marketing, perhaps? I also saw the advertisement you are referring to and took time to read it twice. I guess that is the idea.

Also, it sounds very positive stated this way. It could have been advertised as "Normally, $49.95; now on sale for $39.95."

Is this pool a rip-off?

Q: I've been approached by an acquaintance to join a lottery club and I'd like your opinion of it. Apparently someone is trying to set up groups of 20 people in pools to play our state lottery. Each person pays $60 a year to join and for that receives membership in one of these groups of 20 people. $52 of the fee is used to buy 20 lotto chances each week for 52 weeks, and the remaining $8 goes for "overhead" and "operating expenses." Whatever money is won each week is divided among the 20 group members at the end of the year, minus 10% of total winnings which goes to the organizer of the pool. So what do you think? Shall I join this lottery club, or is it just another rip-off? I value your opinion.

A: I am aware of several similar lottery "clubs." I don't have a very high opinion of them. Here's why.

First, you are joining a group of strangers, or, at best, "acquaintances." It makes more sense to join, or form, a lottery pool where the members already have some common bond. Perhaps they all work together, are neighbors, friends, or family members. There are always fewer problems and more fun when pool members already know each other.

Second, why pay over 12% ($8) of your membership fee for "overhead" and "operating expenses"? That's foolish. Besides, pool expenses are minimal, if they exist at all. This sounds like the place where the organizer plans to make a profit.

Third, winnings should not be held for a year before they are disbursed. There is no reason for holding winnings longer than a month.

Fourth, what is this foolishness about the organizer receiving 10% of pool winnings? That's more than what any member will receive. All pool winnings should go to pool members. Period.

My advice is to pass on this "opportunity" and form your own pool. I think you'll be glad you did.

What about calling those 900 lottery lines to get "high probability" lotto numbers to play?

Q: What do you think of these lottery hotlines that are popping up all over where you can call a 900 number and find out what the numbers are that will have the highest probability of being drawn for your state's lotto game?

A: Not much.

First, these are not lottery services, they are money-making businesses that make money by keeping you on the telephone as long as possible. Usually you pay a minimum of $2.95 for the first minute, and then a lesser amount for each additional minute. The problem is that frequently you must stay on the line for many minutes in order to get the information you desire, and sometimes the material is presented in such a way (hard to understand or too fast) that you are required to call back two or three times in order to get the information you want.

Second, these "high probability" numbers are merely numbers that for short periods of time seem to have come up more often than other numbers. That does not mean they will ever come up again. Remember, chance is at work in lotto drawings, and you cannot predict chance.

Third, what if these numbers you are given were to get drawn? Thousands of other people were also given those same numbers to play, so you'd have to share your winnings with those thousands of other people. Not much chance you'd receive much prize money, probably not even what it cost you for the 900 number call.

And finally, think about it. If people really believed in their "high probability" numbers, they wouldn't share those numbers by telephone, or any other way, at any price. Instead, they'd be playing those numbers, winning millions in every state lottery and keeping it all. At the moment, my advice is to be suspicious of anybody who wants to tell you what the winning lottery numbers are likely to be.

Are discount lottery tickets a good deal?

Q: Not long ago I was approached by someone who wanted to sell me lottery discount coupons, which he said would be good for buying lottery tickets for half price for the next two years. It didn't make sense to me so I didn't buy. Did I pass up a good deal?

A: You showed good judgment. You are referring to the latest scam that unscrupulous people are promoting around the country. These con men (and women) are printing up worthless "coupons" that supposedly enable you to buy your state lottery tickets at big discounts for the next couple of years. However, if you did buy the coupons, you couldn't use them. There are no discounts on lottery coupons. Your ticket seller would laugh at you if you presented him your coupon.

In the future, if you are ever approached with "good deals" like this again, check with your ticket retailer before you do anything. He can call your lottery officials immediately and get clarification as to whether the "deal" is on the up-and-up.

Can you help me contact investors interested in a guaranteed winning numbers system?

Q: I bet you haven't gotten a question like this one before. Can you refer me to any rich people who would be willing to invest $1 million in my guaranteed winning lotto numbers system? I am a student of higher mathematics and probability theory and I have figured out a fail-safe system for picking winning lotto numbers. My problem is that in order for it to work I need to buy one million tickets. But if I could buy the million tickets I—and my investor—could win 10 or 20 million dollars every week, guaranteed!

A: It's a good thing for you we didn't bet. You'd have lost. I receive letters like yours frequently and they always get put in the same place—the wastebasket. Why? Because in spite of what you say, there is no system that can predict winning numbers in a random selection lottery game. Unscrupulous people are always claiming to have the "guaranteed" system which they will sell for a fee, but it doesn't work. And by the way, what is your guarantee? If you don't pick the winning numbers after you have bought a million tickets, will you give back the million dollars immediately? Where will you get that million? Sorry, I can't help you get a million dollars. But I know how you *can* get it: play the state lottery and win it.

Are lottery scams a recent phenomenon?

Q: From time to time you warn us about lottery scams and ways that some people use the lottery to separate us from our money. I know that lotteries have been around for a long time, but I am wondering if this lottery "hustling" is largely a sign of our times, or have lotteries always been plagued by people who are trying to make a fast buck off of our lottery playing?

A: When the first colonists settled Jamestown, they were short of cash so they borrowed an idea from their mother country. They got permission from the king to conduct a lottery. In England, lotteries were a way to raise money for a variety of projects.

In a charter granted in 1612, King James (yes, the same guy who sponsored and funded the translation of the King James Bible) issued a warning to the Jamestown colonists not to defraud people who wanted to participate in the lottery. It sounds to me like lottery "scams" were around in the 1600s; otherwise, King James would not have needed to warn the colonists. Apparently human nature is about the same today as it was 400 years ago.

Incidentally, lotteries conducted by the Jamestown colonists raised about 8,000 pounds sterling each year for the Jamestown settlement. Most of that money was used to pay men and women to travel to Jamestown from England.

What is a good lottery program for my computer?

Q: I recently acquired a computer and a lottery program where the information is loaded with the number of times each number came up a winner in the past. Apparently the calculating is done based on this information. It doesn't seem to take into consideration the trend of numbers as they come out each week. I am looking for a more versatile program. Can you tell me what is considered a good lottery program and where it may be available?

A: There are literally hundreds of lottery programs available for your home computer. Any computer software store will have dozens of them for sale ranging from $19 to $199. I don't recommend any of them because I think they are all selling something that they can't deliver. They all say, or imply, that they enable users to pick future lottery winning numbers. Supposedly, because they analyze past winning (and losing) numbers, they will reveal "patterns" of hot and cold numbers and guide you into selecting winning numbers. This "predicting" can't be done. It is only guessing. Random selection of numbers by state lotteries is not subject to *any* prediction, with or without a computer.

But, if you can keep from taking these programs too seriously, sometimes this lottery software is fun to play around with. One of the best of these software packages is called Lotto Leverage. This software is targeted at the home market and offers graphical winning number history analysis, play selection, performance tracking, "play lotto" simulation and history file management features. Using the simulation feature, players can test their lotto number picking strategies against the winning number history file. It actually becomes a lotto game.

How do you get this software? It is available by mail. Call 1-800-829-6881. It is priced at $39.95.

Remember, this is not a recommendation, merely an answer to your question.

Does the mob's system for picking numbers have credibility?

Q: I know that the daily pick-3 game is really just a legalized version of the illegal numbers games that have been around forever, run by various criminal elements. What I have just seen recently is an advertisement for something called "The Mob System," supposedly the mob's secret number system for winning pick-3 games. This "secret" is for sale for $25.95. Is there any credibility to this "secret"?

A: You have got to be kidding. You can't possibly be tempted by something like this. I also saw the ad you were referring to. It says, "Six months ago we found the mob's **secret** number system in an old Chicago attic. We applied it to today's pick-3 games and Wow. Now you can win and have that extra cash you need so badly each week." All you have to do is send 26 bucks. This ad is really bad, is designed to rip off gullible lottery players, and is designed to beat lawsuits. Look at this ad again.

1. It never says what you get for your money. It *implies* that you will receive a winning pick-3 number picking system, but it never says that.

2. It never says that it (whatever the system is that you are sent) will work. It just says "Wow."

3. It never mentions any guarantee or money-back-if-unsatisfied offer.

4. It attributes the origin of this "secret number system" discovery to something called the "mob" probably because the "system" was signed, "The Mob."

5. The mob left this important document in an "old Chicago attic." How appropriate.

6. And the discoverers, nice people that they are, don't plan to run around to all the lottery states, playing pick-3 games, using the Wow System, making millions of dollars in a matter of days. No, they plan to sell this secret to you for only $25.95.

Now tell me, does all this seem credible to you?

How do I select a company to sell me tickets for out-of-state lotteries?

Q: Please give me some information on how to pick a company that sells tickets for out-of-state lotteries. I want to play some of the lotteries in other states where the lotto odds are better than in our state.

A: Here are the names and telephone numbers for two companies that sell lottery tickets for other-state lotteries: Regal Service Bureau, 800-367-9681; Gaming PA, 800-445-6886. This is not a recommendation for either of these companies, just a mention of two companies that have been around for a long time. There are many other companies that periodically surface to sell lottery players tickets in other states. Most of these organizations don't stay around for long, and some have actually disappeared without buying the lottery tickets that their customers have paid for.

You will see advertisements for ticket sales companies from time to time in various publications. Before using them, I encourage you to ask questions and check out these companies to be certain that they have been around for a few years, charge reasonable prices (a charge of $1 extra for each lottery ticket you purchase is customary), give you a paper copy of your ticket number combinations *before* the drawing dates, are clear about how you are notified of any winnings, and tell you how your winnings are collected.

What do you think of this lottery software?

Q: Because you are the only lottery analyst that I am aware of, I want your opinion of this offer I received recently for some computer software for playing the lottery. The information says, in part, "I wanted to inform you about the biggest breakthrough in lottery technology in a century. We are selling a new software product ($89.95 reduced to $49.95) that trains the hidden capacities of a lottery player's brain through highly sensitive feedback which improves the player's ability to perceive the winning numbers. You may think this is some tabloid teaser or scam, but let me assure you that the principles underlying our software have been validated by multi-year studies at leading universities ... We know what we are doing, both from a psychic and lottery perspective ..." Does any of this sound reasonable?

A: No, it doesn't sound reasonable. Although you didn't say so, I assume that you are asking me if you should buy this "breakthrough." I'm familiar with this offer. I received it also. In my opinion, this "new" software program for lottery players is just the latest attempt by "marketeers" to take advantage of a large percentage of lottery players who can only be described as so desperate to win "the big one" that they will buy any product offered to them that claims to have the elusive "secret" of winning, even though common sense says the product is worthless.

Why do I think your product is a waste of money ? Here are a few reasons:

1) I never trust anyone who says "studies at leading universities" and then doesn't mention which studies and which universities. By the way, which universities are "leading" and which are not-so-leading? As some of the readers of this book know, in addition to my research and writing about playing the lottery, I am also a university professor and I know that no legitimate researcher or academician would ever use that expression. In fact, that phrase was invented years ago by advertising executives seeking to give credibility and legitimacy to products that otherwise had no credibility.

2) This computer program appears to be simply a variation of a rather common computer game that has been around for a long time. In the game, players attempt to guess which letter of the alphabet the computer will randomly select next. Depending on how close your letter is to the one selected by the computer, you win points. If you actually guess the letter the computer selects, or a letter close to it, you win several points. The farther away the letter you guess is from the computer's choice, the smaller the number of points you receive. In this software program, when you guess a correct letter, the program generates a lotto number. Eventually, with enough guesses, you've got your lotto numbers to play. The question that comes to mind is, "What's the connection between guessing these letters and turning them into winning lottery numbers?"

3) The promotional materials say that the "intuition accelerator" program in guessing alphabet letters was developed by a psychic researcher and "trains the hidden capacities of your brain through highly sensitive feedback so that you use more of your core intuitive ability to see into the future," thereby en-

abling you to correctly pick winning lottery numbers. However, the materials also say that ". . . we do not know how this works, only that it does work!" Doesn't this mean that any similar computer game already installed on a home computer where the player guesses what letter, number, or object the computer is going to randomly select—and where the computer lets you know if your guess was correct or incorrect (this is the feedback)—will also train the "hidden capacities of your brain" in the same way that this program does?

4) If this is such a foolproof way to win the lottery, why sell it? Instead, why hasn't this company and their "psychic researcher" used it and won millions? The materials declare very honestly (but foolishly) that the president of this company has only won $60 using their own program. That fact doesn't make me want to run right out and purchase it. I've won more than that without using an "intuition accelerator."

5) And finally, playing the lottery is playing a game of randomness. By definition, randomness cannot be predicted. Looking back we can track winning numbers, and we can sometimes see patterns of winning numbers, but we still cannot assume that those "patterns" of winning numbers will continue into the future because they never do. Lottery officials never worry that computer programs that track or predict winning numbers will ruin their business by producing too many winners.

When people ask me what the secret to winning the lottery is, I suggest they throw a dart at numbers, see where it lands, and play those numbers. The win rate will be at least as high as with any computerized number selection.

What are they really selling?

Q: I read a classified ad the other day that offered a computer program that could be used on my home computer. The ad promised the program would enable me to "beat any lottery or lotto game." It further stated that it cost $99.95, but that I

could purchase it for only $19.95 if I promised to pay the company selling the program 1% of everything I win over $1,000,000 while using it. Are you familiar with this offer? What do you think?

A: I have a bridge I'd like to talk to you about buying . . . .

Yes, I've seen those ads. What this really amounts to is another creative way to sell you a $19.95 software program that picks random numbers. Saying that it is discounted because the company chooses to share in your good fortune when you win is pretty slick. It does create a favorable impression initially— until you think about it.

First, winning lottery numbers are selected randomly. It is impossible to figure out (with or without a computer) which numbers will be selected each week. If you wanted to, you could choose your weekly numbers by pulling numbered pieces of paper out of a paper bag and your chances of getting the winning lottery numbers would be just as good as if you had used a computer to randomly choose your numbers.

Now, what about this wonderful offer of a reduced price if you are willing to share a bit of your winnings? Think about it. If this company really believed its program would enable a player to win, would it be selling it for any amount of money, let alone $19.95? No way! It wouldn't be selling computer programs, it would be using them in every state lottery, winning millions of dollars every week!

How do you play lotto for free?

Q: I have seen an advertisement appearing in the classified ads in my local newspaper for the past few weeks that says, "Earn up to $20,000 a month showing people how to play lotto for free." It gives me a telephone number to call, but no one answers my calls. Can you tell me anything about this? I'm not

so much interested in the job as I am interested in finding out how to play lotto for free.

A: Believe me, you can't play lotto for free, no matter what the ad says.

What you have discovered is another "multi-level marketing" plan tied to lottery ticket sales. This scam has been around for a few years, but I called the telephone number you sent me just to see if anything had changed. Nothing had. After many tries, I managed to find someone home in the evening. Your telephone calls weren't answered because you called during the day—that's reasonable—and the two men who live there work at real jobs during the day.

The first person I talked to told me that "for only $25" I could become a member of a nationwide lottery playing club that buys lotto tickets in various states for its members. For this membership fee, members receive a monthly newsletter, a "free" 64-page book and 12 "free" lottery tickets every month for some state lottery in the country.

Oh yes, you get to select the numbers for your 12 tickets.

If one of your numbers wins something, the rest of the members share 50 percent, your "sponsor" (the person who sold you your membership) receives 25 percent and you receive 25 percent.

When I pushed and kept asking who paid for these 12 "free" lottery tickets each month, because states do not give free tickets, I was handed over to a roommate because "he can explain better how everything works."

He tried. He even tried to tell me that the club was so large it got substantial discounts from every state lottery because the club bought tickets in large quantities. I pointed out that was illegal—and impossible.

Finally he remembered the $25 fee that is automatically deducted from members' checking accounts every month.

Your 12 "free" lottery tickets cost you $25 each month and you get to share your winnings.

Such a deal.

Oh yes, you earn that "$20,000 a month" by selling others the same membership you buy, and you receive $5 per month out of his or her monthly $25 fee. When the person you sell a membership to in turn sells someone else, you get $4 a month from that sale, and so on, $3, $2, $1 for five levels of sales.

And that is what that ad is all about.

Just in case you are wondering, no, I didn't join the club.

Should I play the German lottery?

Q: I just received a solicitation in the mail to play the Northwest German State Lottery. It is really confusing to read and I confess that I don't understand how it works, but the brochure says that one out of every three people who enter will be a winner. It is rather expensive to play, from $148 for a quarter ticket to $541 for a whole ticket, but I am tempted to try anyway. After all, the odds of winning are 1 in 3 and you are paid in one lump-sum payment when you win. That certainly beats the odds in my state lottery. It almost sounds too good to be true. What do you think?

A: It is too good to be true, but I think that if you have money to waste, you should do it, buy a ticket. Some people learn best the hard way.

On the other hand, if you have any common sense at all, you will think about what you read next.

First, that solicitation to play the German lottery is illegal and the company in Canada that mailed it to you (and others like it soliciting for lotteries in other countries) knowingly broke the law. Also, if you decide to mail in your money to play the German lottery as the solicitation directs you, you will be violating U.S. postal regulations and you too will be breaking the law.

Secondly, why would you want to play a lottery in another country anyway, especially when you don't understand how it is played? I know, you believe that the odds are so much better than in your state lottery, but you are wrong. Let's assume that what the brochure says is true, that there are only 1.5 million tickets sold each week and that 600,000 of them will be picked as winners, which means that the odds of winning are better than 1 in 3. That's true, but what you don't understand is that each one of these 1.5 million tickets costs $541 *each* and very few people buy a whole ticket. Since each ticket can be divided into four parts, most people buy one quarter of a ticket. If that ticket wins, they split the prize four ways. And, let me point out to you something that the brochure failed to mention: the top prizes are small and there aren't many of them. For the 26 weekly drawings, there are only 10 weeks where there is a prize of over $1 million, and the largest jackpot during those 10 weeks is $3.7 million. So, what that actually means is that the odds of winning one of these 10 weekly top prizes is 1 in 1.5 million, not 1 in 3. And it gets worse. The brochure didn't point out that 16 of those 26 weekly drawings only have a top prize of $625,000. For these 16 weeks the chances of winning one of these 16 top prizes is also 1 in 1.5 million.

Think about it. If you took that same $541 and spread it out over 26 weeks ($20 a week) playing Florida's Lotto where the weekly jackpot begins at $7 million—five times the size of the usual German Lottery grand prize—your chances of winning the Florida jackpot would be 1 in 700,000, twice as good as the German Lottery odds of 1.5 million.

What you actually are buying with your $541 is a very good chance (1 in 3) of winning one of the thousands of weekly small prizes. Do you really want to spend $541 for a chance to do that? You could spend the same amount in your state lottery each week and stand a much better chance of winning a large prize amount. If you want 1-in-3 odds, play the scratch-off games in your state.

I've said it before: stay away from playing out-of-country lotteries, including the Canadian and Australian lotteries. They are all bad deals compared to U.S. lotteries.

Is there software designed for lottery pools?

Q: We have an office lottery pool at the place where I work that has won small amounts a few times, and I am responsible for the collecting of money and the record keeping. Since there are about 40 of us who contribute to the pool, sometimes the record keeping gets to be very time consuming. Do you know of any IBM-compatible computer software that is designed for group lottery ticket buying and record keeping? I suspect I could make my job a lot easier if I had some computerized help.

A: A software program called "Office Lottery Manager" is IBM-compatible and is designed for automated record keeping for up to 150 players in a pool. It keeps track of purchases, balances, and winnings and allows players to choose their own numbers, or it can keep track of and select the most frequently winning numbers—or even the numbers that are seldom winners.

The cost is $49.95, and to order you call 1-604-384-8310. Remember, this is not a recommendation, just an answer to your question.

What is a "no risk" lottery?

Q: I keep seeing an advertisement in the magazines I read for a "no risk" lottery. Have you seen it? Do you know anything about it? It says that if you play, "you get a full refund on the face amount of your entries whether you win or lose." It also says that there is only a one-time entry, which you can keep playing for as long as you want because you are automatically entered in each week's drawing, and you can win again and again off the same entry. When you win, the ad says, your winnings are paid in one lump sum, and the winnings are guaranteed by a "stable foreign government." How is it possible for a lottery like this to exist? It almost makes me want to spend the

$10 to get their report on how all of this happens. What do you think?

A: How is it possible for a lottery like this, in which everyone wins, to exist? It's not possible.

This is just another of the many lottery scams that promise gullible people what can't be delivered. If you were foolish enough to send in your $10 for the promised "report," you would find that what you really get if you participate is not what you thought you were promised.

Think about it. Lotteries are set up by states and "stable foreign governments" to make money for the state or the government, not to make every player a winner. The only way that lotteries can continue to operate is if most people lose and only a few win. It has to take in more money from losers than it pays out to winners. The minute the lottery doesn't make a profit, it will cease operating.

Besides, I keep reminding people, if someone or some group really has a guaranteed winning system, why sell that secret for $10? Why not be selfish and use it to win millions, rather than going to all the work and cost to promote, advertise and sell the "secret" for a few bucks? Keep your money. Spend it on your state lottery games. It will be better spent.

PART IV

So That's How It Works!

"I got this offer in the mail today to play the Canadian lottery, but there are a few things that I'm a bit confused about."

Does the lottery's quick pick number selection computer give the same set of numbers to more than one person?

Q: Just how random is a state lottery computer's quick pick random number selection? Does this keep everyone else from getting the numbers that were selected for me by the computer?

A: In November of 1992, a $28 million lotto jackpot in Virginia was won by five winners, each of whom had the six winning numbers—and each ticket had been selected by the Virginia Lottery's Easy Pick system. Since then I have received a sizable quantity of mail from players who ask the same question: "How did five players receive the same six numbers by playing Easy Pick?"

Apparently, many lottery players think that the different state lotteries' quick pick systems prevent anyone from having the same six numbers. That is not what happens.

When you play lotto or any of the lottery games in which the lottery computer picks your numbers for you, your numbers are selected at random, not in any predetermined order. Each store's computerized lottery terminal has its own random number generator. This "randomizer" inside the terminal determines your quick pick selection using a complex series of mathematical formulas. The terminal does not "remember" what numbers have been selected previously and does not "know" what numbers have been selected at other terminal locations. Because it's random, it is possible for a quick pick system to pick the same numbers for more than one player.

Why does the lottery pay lotto jackpot winners over a period of years, not in one payment?

Q: You have probably answered this question before, but I still don't know what the answer is and my friends and I have been doing some serious speculation about it. If you win the lotto jackpot, the state pays you your winnings spread over a number of years. Why? We can't figure out why, other than the state wanting to use your money and the interest it earns over the years.

A: First, not all state lotteries pay their lotto winners over a period of years. A few states now offer their players a choice of taking half of the jackpot amount in a lump sum or collecting the entire jackpot amount over a period of years, but the majority of states still spread payments over 20 years, or even over 25 years.

The reason state lotteries spread out payments in this manner is because there isn't enough money to pay you all at once when you win, so an annuity is used to pay you the total over time.

This annuity (an annuity is a fixed interest savings account for a specified number of years) must accumulate enough interest so that annual payments can be made that will eventually total the winning jackpot amount. Why is that?

Most of us don't stop to think about all of the money that must be paid out of every lotto jackpot. In most lottery states, of the total lottery ticket sales each week, by legislative mandate about 35% goes into the state treasury, 10% goes for ticket and administrative expenses, and 5% is paid as ticket sales commissions. The remaining 50% of ticket sales goes into the prize pool. This prize pool total is what you hear advertised as the jackpot amount each week.

What most of us forget is that same jackpot prize pool must also pay second-, third-, and fourth-prize winners—and they must be paid immediately.

For example, let's assume that the jackpot this week in the Florida Lottery is advertised as $10 million. From that same pool that offers a first prize of $10 million, the state will pay $1.3 million (13%) to second-prize winners who select five out of six numbers; $1.9 million (19%) to third-prize winners who select four of six numbers; and $1.8 million (18%) to fourth-prize winners who select three of six numbers.

Thus, from a prize pool of $10 million, $5 million (50%) is paid immediately to second-, third-, and fourth-prize winners, leaving only $5 million to pay the grand-prize winner who won $10 million!

Do you see the problem? The lottery can't afford to pay you your jackpot all at once. There is just not enough money.

Is it legal to cash in a winning lottery ticket you find?

Q: What would happen if a person loses a winning lottery ticket and someone else finds it and cashes it in? Could the finder go to jail?

A: No, the person would not go to jail, unless it was proven that he or she stole the ticket from the rightful owner. Finding an unsigned, winning lottery ticket is the same as finding money.

A lottery ticket is considered a bearer instrument. The person who brings it to the lottery is considered the owner. If you haven't signed your ticket, it is like losing cash. It is a good idea to sign your ticket as soon as you know it's a winner. Then, if you lose it, you have a better chance of proving it belongs to you if it is found. State lotteries are not responsible for determining ownership of lost, stolen or destroyed tickets.

Can lottery drawings be rigged?

Q: How do we know that the drawings we see on television are not rigged in some way? Wouldn't it be fairly easy to tamper with the drawing machines or the numbered balls?

A: No, it would be impossible to rig a drawing in any way in a state lottery. There is just too much security. In fact, one of the security measures is to televise the drawings so that players can see what goes on.

Although procedures vary slightly from state to state, all state lotteries follow pretty much the same pre-drawing procedures while in the presence of lottery officials and lottery security at every stage:

1. The set of balls to be used in the drawing is randomly selected from among several sets of balls.

2. The drawing machine is randomly selected from among several machines.

3. Balls are individually measured and weighed to ensure that they meet certain standards.

4. The balls are loaded into the drawing machine while in a "secure room," a special room at the television station that is kept locked and is for lottery use only.

5. A series of pretests—drawings—are conducted to see if anything unusual occurs. If nothing unusual occurs, such as a pattern of balls being drawn repeatedly, all is ready for the drawing.

6. Lottery security officials, lottery personnel, and external auditors stand by. No one is permitted near the drawing machine until the television drawing.

7. The drawing host or hostess conducts the drawing.

8. Winning numbers are called in to the media and to the lottery's data center.

Do free tickets ever win, or are they free because they won't win?

Q: Occasionally, state lotteries offer a free lottery ticket or two when you purchase so many tickets. However, I haven't heard of anyone winning with a free ticket, and I know that I certainly haven't come close with the free tickets I've received. Is it possible that the free tickets are ones that the lottery officials know are non-winning tickets, so it is safe to give them away because there will be no winners?

A: My, you have a suspicious mind. No, state lotteries do not give away worthless, non-winning free tickets. If any state lottery did such a thing, it would destroy the confidence of millions of lottery players and they would cease to play the lottery. Every state lottery works hard to maintain a squeaky-clean, above-reproach image.

Besides, thousands of lottery players have won prizes using their free tickets. For example, Albert Georges, a Minnesota Lottery player, purchased five tickets in hopes of winning millions in the Minnesota Lottery's Pick-6 game, Powerball. When he bought his five tickets, he also received a free ticket for the pick-5 game, Gopher 5. Albert didn't win anything in the Powerball drawing, but guess what—his free Gopher 5 ticket won him $100,000! After taxes were withheld, Albert took home a check for $72,000. Not bad for a free ticket.

Can expired winning scratch-off tickets still be turned in?

Q: I was rummaging through my junk drawer the other day and came across a couple of old winning instant game tickets that I never got around to turning in and forgot about. One ticket is worth $2 and the other won $5. The problem is that the instant games these tickets are from are no longer being played. Is there any chance that I could sweet-talk my lottery ticket retailer into giving me the money for them anyway? Or perhaps I could send them directly to the lottery itself and receive the money that way. After all, I'm sure the money has been set aside to pay for these tickets. Any advice?

A: Yes. My advice is never put winning lottery tickets in a junk drawer—or anywhere. Cash them immediately.

You wouldn't believe haw many people have winning instant game tickets for small amounts of money but never get around to cashing them. The Virginia Lottery, for example, reported that for 25 of its different instant games there were 1,328,138 winning tickets sold with cash prizes worth $567,891,241, but only 1.1 million winning tickets were cashed in! That's 200,000 tickets, or about 18% of all winning tickets, which have not been cashed in and are probably lying around in drawers, wallets, and cookie jars.

Some of these winning tickets may yet be cashed in. The problem is that when a lottery stops selling a specific instant game it sets a time limit for cashing in that game's winning tickets. The time limit varies from state to state. Some states allow three months, six months, or even up to one year after the end of the game for cashing in winning tickets. But, in all states, once that deadline is reached, there is no cashing in of tickets permitted, no matter how much "sweet-talking" you do.

And you are correct about the lottery setting aside the prize money for you, but not forever. After the deadline passes, the prize money that had been set aside by the lottery to pay those winning tickets is put back into the prize pool or used by the lottery in some other way.

What you ought to do immediately is run your winning tickets over to your ticket agent and see if you can still cash them. Perhaps the time limit has not expired. If it has, there is no chance of collecting.

What can be done to keep investment groups from winning jackpots?

Q: What are state lotteries doing to keep huge investment groups like the one from Australia that won the Virginia $27 million jackpot from doing the same thing again whenever there is a giant jackpot?

A: When the Virginia Lottery jackpot reached $27 million, a group of investors from Australia wired $7 million to a bank in Virginia in an attempt to buy every one of the seven million number combinations. With the help of couriers and others taking money and play slips to retailers, and by tying up the ticket printing machines at some stores for days, the group was able to buy about five million of the seven million possible combinations for the drawing before their time ran out. In this case, five million tickets was enough to win the $27 million jackpot.

The Virginia Lottery, like the other state lotteries, was quick to assure players that this large block sale of tickets would not happen again. New regulations were put into effect immediately.

The new regulations that Virginia and other states are instituting include limits on the amount of time any one customer can tie up a ticket terminal. "Prompt service" to lottery customers is required. Also, limits are being placed on the maximum number of tickets one store may sell for one drawing. This will prohibit giant blocks of tickets from being sold at any one store and force huge ticket purchases to be spread over hundreds of different stores. This will effectively prohibit any one group from being able to purchase all the possible number combinations for any drawing.

If it is not possible to buy all the possible number combinations, investor groups are not likely to risk their money on the lottery. The Australian group was very lucky. With all their planning and organization, they thought that they had enough time to buy all seven million possible number combinations, but they ran out of time and only managed to purchase five million. The winning ticket could very easily have been among the two million tickets they were not able to purchase.

What happens to my ENTRY tickets?

Q: I wonder if you could give me some information on ENTRY tickets. I received two of them recently while playing our scratch-off games and sent them in, but I never found out what happened. I have never seen a pamphlet or anything to tell players what the lottery does with these tickets when they get them, or how long they are good for. I never see anything in the paper about ENTRY drawings, and I don't have any idea of what might be happening with them. I would appreciate your comments on these ENTRY drawings.

A: You are not the only lottery player who is puzzled by ENTRY tickets and how they are handled. I receive letters like yours from players in every lottery state, all wondering why their state lottery doesn't inform players what is happening with these ENTRY tickets. Generally, state lotteries do a good job of informing players about every little aspect of playing lottery games, but for some reason, the state lotteries don't seem to make any significant effort to tell you about ENTRY drawings.

Every state lottery handles these ENTRY contests a bit differently, but, for the most part, this is what happens: Lottery officials like to keep these second chance contests running all year long because it helps keep people playing the scratch-off games even when they are not winning. When you scratch off your ticket and find that you haven't won any money but have won an ENTRY ticket, you feel like a winner—even though you haven't won anything. Consequently, you are likely to keep playing and buying more tickets.

Meanwhile, when you get an ENTRY ticket you sign the back of your ticket and send it into the lottery headquarters where it is put into a huge pool of other ENTRY tickets. Generally, it takes from six to ten weeks to get a sufficient number of tickets collected (anywhere from 100,000 to 500,000) so that a drawing can be held. At that drawing, sometimes televised but usually not, a small number of tickets (from six to twelve) are drawn from that pool of thousands. At that point, the owners of the ENTRY tickets that were drawn are notified that they have become "finalists." All the rest of the nonwinning ENTRY tickets in that drawing pool are disposed of, and a new drawing and pool is begun by the lottery. Sometimes the owners of the tickets that were drawn are given a small prize at that point, and then they go to the final round of drawings, or to a roulette-like "Big Spin" game. This next drawing is held within the next few weeks and is only for the few owners of the tickets that were drawn. These lucky entrants are guaranteed to win a substantial chunk of money, sometimes as much as $1 million.

What it boils down to is that if you have not been notified by telephone and registered mail that you are a winner within two months of sending in your ENTRY tickets, you were not a lucky "second chance" winner and your ENTRY ticket has been thrown away.

Am I legally liable for not buying lottery tickets as promised?

Q: I have an agreement with my sister who lives in another state to play the lotteries of both our states. Each week, each of us is supposed to buy 10 lotto tickets with certain sets of agreed-upon numbers for our two states' lotteries. If either of us wins, we are then supposed to share. My sister dutifully buys the tickets each week for her state lottery—that's $520 a year—and splits with me when she occasionally wins small amounts. Actually, she has sent me $114 so far this year as my share of her lottery winnings. The problem is, I don't buy any lottery tickets for my state lottery, she only thinks I do. I just pocket the $520 a year that I'm supposed to spend instead of just wasting the money each week on a gamble that has such poor odds. Periodically, I tell her that we have three of six numbers, and then I send her $2 or $3 as her "prize" share out of my own pocket. It keeps her happy. My question is, if our numbers did happen to hit for the big jackpot in my state lottery, and I haven't played our numbers, am I legally liable to my sister for her share of the prize money that she didn't win?

A: I hope so. I'm not an attorney and don't know for sure, but I'd be glad to bet that you are liable if your sister chose to take you to court. After all, you have an agreement, money has changed hands based on that agreement, and you both have a history of operating based on that agreement. If I were the judge or on the jury, I'd throw the book at you. In fact, if I knew who your sister was, I'd call her and recommend that she become the first sister in the country to file for divorce from her brother. I think she has grounds and would be better off without you.

Surprisingly enough to most of us who would never even think of being so dishonest with another person, let alone with a member of our family, there are many cases just like yours that I am aware of. In almost all cases, however, they end up tragically. I am reminded of the case of the husband who went to the horse races every Thursday evening for years. His wife never went with him, but she always gave him $10 to bet for her on some horse that she'd picked out. The husband usually didn't bet her money on her pick because he "knew" she didn't know what she was doing. Instead, he'd bet her money on a horse of his choice and simply told her that her choice didn't win. Then one day she picked a horse for him to bet on for her—and it won. Not only did it win, it was a 99 to 1 longshot. Sure enough, that was the time she decided to check for herself to find out how her horse had done. By the time her husband got home, she was ecstatic because she had had lots of time to think about how to spend all her winnings. That marriage didn't last too much longer.

You might want to think about the possibility of getting caught and what the implications might be. Besides, are you really so hard up that you have to rip off your sister for a few bucks over the possibility (a real long shot at that) of winning a lottery jackpot?

Do size and weight of ping-pong balls affect numbers drawn?

Q: Many lotteries pick their numbers by using balls in drawing machines. Isn't it possible for those balls to be slightly different sizes and to weigh different amounts, even infinitesimally different amounts, and if so, wouldn't that affect which numbers bounced into the selection slots? I'm just curious. Perhaps players should play certain numbers based on the differences in the weight and the size of the balls. What do you think?

A: I think that you are grasping at straws. Why not just pick some numbers, have fun anticipating winning, and treat the lottery the way it was designed—as a series of games?

However, some people do support your speculation and have suggested that studying lottery balls can make you a big lottery winner, but, then again, some people believe that their pets can pick winning numbers. I don't think that either group stand much chance of winning unless they are just plain lucky like all the rest of the winners before them.

Nearly all lotteries operate in the following manner, or something very similar, when it comes to their lottery drawing equipment, including their sets of bouncing balls.

Each night, in preparation for the nightly drawing, all balls are weighed and measured by a team of three people. These people even wear gloves when handling balls prior to a drawing so that no oils or residue from their skin can contaminate the balls. The weight of each ball must be within .008 of a gram standard. The size must be exact as well.

Lottery security officials make sure that all balls are painted exactly the same. The balls, for example, all have two digits on them. Balls 1 through 9 are painted 01 through 09. This ensures that approximately the same amount of paint is on each ball so there is no difference in weight or wind resistance. A line has been painted under each number on the balls in order for observers to distinguish between similar looking numbers that could be viewed upside down (06 and 09, for example, or 01 and 10). Since each ball has the line painted under the digits, and not just painted under balls with numbers that might be confused at first glance, no one ball has any additional weight caused by the presence of the additional painted line.

Several sets of balls are on hand for each drawing. A random selection is made before the drawing to determine which set will be used that night. The machines that hold the balls are also determined randomly prior to the drawing. Several test drawings are held before the actual live drawing, to be sure that the balls are being drawn in a random fashion and that the machine is operating properly. If any irregularity is seen, another machine or a different set of balls can be substituted in the live drawing.

An independent external auditor is present throughout the entire procedure—before, during, and after each drawing. Officials from the lottery's security and marketing divisions perform all testing under the watchful eyes of the auditor.

All of these precautions don't leave any room for playing numbers based on the differences in balls.

Is it really a criminal act to transport a lottery ticket across a state line?

Q: Do you want to hear something really crazy? We don't have a lottery yet here in Mississippi so those of us who want to play the lottery have to buy lottery tickets from other state lotteries. I was particularly excited when our neighboring state, Louisiana, voted in the lottery. Since I live only eight miles for Louisiana, it would be very convenient to run across the state line and pick up my lottery tickets. But guess what? If I do that, I will become a criminal. In their wisdom, our state legislators have created a new law that will make it illegal for Mississippi residents to buy out-of-state lottery tickets and bring them back home. Possessing an out-of-state lottery ticket in Mississippi will be a misdemeanor. Can you believe that foolishness?

A: You are right, that's really crazy.

Obviously, Mississippi politicians are futilely trying to keep Mississippi dollars from being spent in other states. And it won't work. People will still buy the out-of-state lottery tickets. Mississippi will eventually realize that it needs its own state lottery and this crazy law should speed up the process of creating it.

Can a business buy lottery tickets—and collect if the tickets win?

Q: I'd like your opinion on something. I am the president of a small manufacturing corporation with about 50 employees. Recently, I have been thinking about buying 100 lottery tickets each week with company money. My thinking is that spending this much money each week (which I couldn't afford to do out of my own pocket) would certainly increase my chances of winning. Winning a large jackpot would be a real boost for my company and would enable us to expand. If these tickets didn't win the jackpot, but instead won smaller amounts, I would use whatever winnings we did receive for employee bonuses and benefits of some sort. My question is, can a business legally be a winner of the lottery, or do you have to be an individual to win?

A: Yes, a business can be a lottery winner and collect winnings in the name of the business. It happens relatively often. In 1992—and five months after the drawing—the owner of a winning $19.4 million Missouri Lottery jackpot came forward to collect the prize, and the winner was a corporation, Royale Marketing, Inc., of Clayton, Missouri. Royale Marketing is a general marketing firm. Royale Marketing's jackpot at that time was the second largest jackpot in Missouri Lottery history. The president of the corporation, Ruth Bender, who collected the first annual payment of approximately $970,000 before taxes (and there will be 19 more of these!) said that the corporation has, on an infrequent basis in the past, purchased lottery tickets. This particular ticket was purchased by a company shareholder on behalf of the corporation.

What are your chances of doing the same thing for your company? Not very good. The chances of winning the lottery with your 100 tickets a week are not really a whole lot better than if you were purchasing 10 tickets a week, so don't get your hopes up that the lottery is the answer to your expansion problems. Let me illustrate. In your state's 6/49 game there are 13,983,816 different number combinations. After you buy 10 tickets, there are still 13,983,806 number combinations that could include the winning numbers. If you buy 100 tickets, ten times as many, you are still left with 13,983,716 number combinations that may include the winner. There is not a lot of difference between buying 10 tickets and 100 tickets when it comes to increasing your chances of winning.

Where can we find guidelines on forming a family lottery club?

Q: Several of my family members and I want to form a lottery club where each of us puts in a few dollars each week to buy lottery tickets, and then if we win we will all share. But we need a little help doing this. Can you recommend any book or publication that gives guidelines for this sort of thing? I understand it is pretty much a simple thing to do, but since we are all family members, I want to be certain that we do it right so that we don't make mistakes and cause any hard feelings.

A: You have the right attitude about forming a lottery pool. Set it up correctly from the beginning and you will avoid the possibility of problems (sometimes major ones) should your pool be lucky and win a substantial jackpot. You should also be aware that different states treat lottery clubs differently in terms of paying prizes to pool members. You will want to know what your state lottery guidelines are. And don't forget the IRS. They have some "suggestions" for lottery clubs also.

There is a good book entitled *WIN MILLION$$ PLAYING*

THE LOTTERY: How to Form a Lottery Club and Win Your Share of Million$ by Michael P. Burke. This simply written and easily understood book will tell you everything you need to know in order to form and run a successful lottery club.

Another reason I like to recommend this book is that the author successfully practices what he preaches, and that's not too common when it comes to people who write about winning the lottery. Mike formed a lottery club several years ago and his club has come close to winning the grand prize several times. The most recent time was for the January 29, 1994, drawing of the Florida Lottery. Mike's lottery club had one 5-of-6 winning ticket and multiple 3- and 4-of-6 tickets. This is the seventh time Mike's club has hit five out of the six numbers. When was the last time any of us hit five out of six playing by ourselves?

WIN MILLION$$ PLAYING THE LOTTERY is available from Kennesaw Mountain Publishing, Inc., P.O. Box 440369, Kennesaw, GA 30144 for $12.95 (Postpaid).

Is sending lottery tickets by mail still against the law?

Q: While buying my lottery tickets the other day I noticed a rack of special occasion greeting cards that were designed to hold a lottery ticket as a gift. These gift cards have humorous messages in them and are really kind of cute. I bought three of the cards and three lottery tickets to put in them. I am planning to send them to my three "secret pals" as little surprise gifts. However, I just thought of something. Isn't sending lottery tickets through the mail against the law? Has this changed? Is that why these lottery tickets gift cards are now available?

A: Sending lottery tickets, or any other lottery materials, through the mail is still against the law. You may send lottery tickets by way of Federal Express-type services, however, and that is perfectly legal. It's just the U.S. Postal Service that is out of bounds.

The new lottery ticket gift cards are a great idea for those of us who like to give lottery tickets as presents, and you will soon find them in most convenience stores or in other establishments that sell lottery tickets.

Will you get in trouble if you mail them to your "pals"? Probably not because the post office will not know what you have inside your envelope when it is mailed, although I encourage you to find another way to deliver your cards to your friends. Millions of people routinely send lottery tickets through the mail because they do not know that it is against the law, and the postal authorities do nothing. I know of companies trying to sell U.S. residents foreign lottery tickets by mail that have been charged with violating the law, but I know of no individual who has been charged with violating this law—ever. I think the post office also believes that it is a stupid law and doesn't run around looking for violators. In the meantime, you might drop a note to your elected representatives in Congress suggesting that they take another look at this atavistic law.

Are winners permitted to sell remaining annual payments?

Q: If a jackpot winner wants to sell remaining annual payments to someone else for a lump-sum amount, is he or she permitted to do so? Some of us wouldn't live to collect 20 years of winnings and could use the money now.

A: It hasn't been permitted in the past, and lotteries generally don't encourage the practice, but the courts are increasingly saying that lottery winners have the right to do so and that lotteries must comply with the winners' request because the winner owns the prize.

Thurman Garrison, of Fairmont, West Virginia, won $250,000 paid over 20 years. After taxes, he received about $10,000 a year.

In December of 1990, he sold his annuity to Stone Street Capital, Inc., of Upper Marlboro, Maryland, for $88,120. He paid off bills, fixed up the house, and still had some money to invest. He was happy with the deal.

The people who buy the annuities typically are investors who want a secure investment for a number of years.

Are losing tickets tax deductible?

Q: I have saved all my losing scratch-off, pick-3, pick-4, pick-5 and lotto tickets. Can I use these losing tickets as tax deductions?

A: Losing lottery tickets can be used as deductions to offset winnings for the same year in which they were purchased. If you win the jackpot in 1995 for example, and you have $432 in losing tickets in 1995, you can offset $432 as gambling losses on your tax return for 1995. You can offset other lottery winnings with losing tickets as well. For example, if you win $1,000 in the instant games, you can use other losing tickets to reduce the taxes on that amount. Gambling losses are not deductible unless you win, and then only up to the amount of your winnings.

Can Canadians play U.S. lotteries, win and collect those winnings?

Q: I live in a small town in Canada, about 15 miles from Vancouver. I play the Canadian Lottery a lot but I have never played a U.S. lottery because I thought that it was illegal for a Canadian citizen to go to one of the states and purchase a lottery ticket. Recently a friend told me that I was wrong. Am I? I hope so because I am about to take a long trip starting in Washington state and ending up in Florida. I will be going through several lottery states and would like to be able to play those lotteries which, by the way, usually have much bigger weekly jackpots than our provincial lotteries. Also, if it is legal for me to buy American lottery tickets, and I win, how would I—a Canadian citizen—go about collecting my winnings? I'm sorry if these questions sound stupid to you, but I get conflicting answers when I ask people around here.

A: Your questions are not stupid. Readers of this book do not ask stupid questions.

Simply stated, it is legal for you to buy lottery tickets from U.S. lotteries, as long as you don't violate U.S. postal regulations by purchasing them through the mail. You certainly may visit states and play those state lotteries, and you may collect your winnings when you are lucky enough to win. It's not a big, complicated problem to collect from U.S. lotteries. Although each state is slightly different in its rules for redeeming winning tickets, small wins are usually paid to you by the retailer who sells you the lottery tickets. You may have to collect big wins, those worth over a few hundred dollars, from a local or regional lottery office nearby. Just ask for the location of the regional office at any retailer who sells lottery tickets. And good luck.

What happens when a lottery winner dies without a will? Who gets the annual lottery payments?

Q: What happens when a person wins the lottery and then dies before he or she collects all of the winnings, doesn't have a will, and doesn't have any relatives? Who gets the uncollected winnings? Does the lottery keep them?

A: The state gets the uncollected winnings if there is no will and no relatives.

Without a will, sometimes even surviving relatives don't get the uncollected winnings because of disputes that arise. Although this doesn't happen very often, it does happen. A bank janitor from Harlem, Solomon Keith, became a rich man overnight after winning the New York Lotto in 1987. But Keith never received all of the $3.8 million prize. He died a year later in a car accident. His remaining annual lottery payments were finally auctioned to pay bills and settle an estate dispute between surviving family members. "Since the week he hit the lotto, I tried to get him to make out a will," said Keith's lawyer, Joel Bernstein. "But ... he was like a little kid, saying 'I'm gonna live forever now.' "

Keith's jackpot brought a winning bid of $2.075 million from Presidential Life Insurance of Nyack, NY.

How do I redeem a winning ticket if I'm no longer in the state?

Q: A couple of weeks ago my husband and I were traveling through Missouri, and while stopped at a gas station we purchased some "5 Card Cash" lottery instant game tickets. We didn't scratch them off immediately, and, in fact, we forgot about them until two nights later when we got back to Louisiana. When we scratched them off we had two winning tickets, one for $50 and one for $25. The problem is that these tickets have to be redeemed at the store where we bought them—and that is back in Missouri. Is there any way we can redeem them without going back to Missouri?

A: As you now know, it is always a good idea to scratch off instant game tickets immediately when you buy them—and collect instantly just so that you don't have a problem collecting winnings, or tickets getting lost or stolen. Every winning lottery ticket is a bearer instrument which may be cashed in by whoever possesses the ticket, signs it and turns it in.

Several lottery states require that a winning ticket be redeemed at the retailer where the winner purchased it. It was set up this way because it is the most cost-efficient way to handle scratcher tickets. The distribution of these tickets and the collection of money generated by them is a very complicated and expensive task. Accounting procedures are simplified when tickets are purchased and redeemed at the same location.

In cases like yours where you cannot return to the retailer from which you bought your ticket, you can still collect. You can either take your ticket to a regional lottery office, which isn't possible for you because you are in another state, or you can mail the ticket in to the lottery and collect your winnings by mail. Players don't like this redemption system, and most states—including Missouri—are trying to change it.

In the meantime, here is what you do. Call the lottery offices and ask for the address to which you should send your ticket. There are several lottery addresses and if you send it to the wrong address, you'll probably never get it cashed. Sign the back of the ticket and photocopy the front and back of the ticket for yourself. Mail the original with your name and address to the lottery address you were given. You should receive a check in about three weeks. And don't delay doing this. Each state has different time limits for collecting on winning tickets. Some states give you up to one year after the game's ending date, while others only give you 60 days.

By the way, you are in good company. On March 3, 1993, Millie Bond of Cameron, Missouri, a laborer in a shoe factory, decided to play the lottery for the first time and bought one lotto ticket. She won a $29.6 million Powerball jackpot. Since then she has discovered the instant games and how much fun they are. Last month, like you, she bought a few "5 Card Cash" tickets, scratched them off and won a free ticket. She took that ticket back, got another one, and this time it was a $5000 winner. Now that's a lady with good luck. She should have started playing years ago.

Is there any way I can still win if I don't have my winning ticket?

Q: Some weeks back I scratched off a lottery ticket and found that I had won $50. I set the scratched ticket aside, intending to cash it in when I went to the store. Unfortunately, my husband came along and saw the scratched ticket on the kitchen counter and, assuming it was a worthless ticket threw it in the fireplace with some other papers and used it to start the fire that evening. My question is, does the lottery have any way of telling which winning scratch-off tickets were sold at each store? I'm wondering if I could still claim the $50 by persuading the lottery that since I know the day it was sold, and since no one else is going to turn it in, I must have purchased it. What do you think?

A: With very rare exceptions, in every state the rule is, "No ticket, no prize." Sorry, you don't stand any chance of collecting.

Here is a similar story to yours, only much sadder. Virginia resident Brenda Phillips and her husband Bucky bought gasoline and a CASH EXPLOSION scratch-off ticket at a retailer at 11 p.m. on July 18, 1993. Brenda was driving, so Bucky began scratching the ticket. He had only scratched the top three firecrackers when the wind took the ticket from his hand and—he thought—blew it out the window. Since it was dark out, they knew they would never find it, so they didn't stop.

Later, when Brenda cleaned out the car, she found the ticket. Apparently it had blown back in the rear window. She saw that Bucky had uncovered one $50,000 in the play area. She said, "I thought you had to choose from the several firecrackers and could only scratch three firecrackers in this game, so when I saw he had already scratched three and they didn't match, I figured he'd lost." Thinking it was a losing ticket, she scratched the rest of the play area and uncovered two more $50,000 symbols. "Too bad," she thought. "If only he had scratched the right three firecrackers!" Still thinking it was a loser, Brenda left the ticket on a table for trash.

When she talked to Bucky later about it, she told him what she had done. He said, "It's a winner!" and wanted to see it. But when they raced to find the ticket they discovered that the ticket had been discarded—and the trash had already been picked up from the curb. With little hope, they hurried to the landfill to look for the ticket.

They never found it.

When legally separated, do half your lottery winnings go to your spouse?

Q: I know that you are not a lawyer and don't give legal advice, but I wonder if you've ever come across this problem before. My wife and I are separated and our divorce should be final in the next two months. Last week I picked 5-out-of-6 numbers in the lottery and won just under $5000 dollars, although I haven't gone to collect it yet. My question is, do half of my winnings belong to my wife? I could certainly use the money now, but I'm thinking of waiting until after the divorce is final before I collect it. Have you heard of other cases like this?

A: You are correct; I don't give legal advice. Call your attorney.

But you may be interested to know that what has happened to you has happened to many other people and frequently with a lot more money at stake. Take the case of Rhode Island lottery winner Dr. Nagib Giha.

Four months before his divorce was to become final, Dr. Giha won $2.4 million. Since the divorce agreement had already been agreed to by both parties, Mr. Giha did not bother to inform his wife of his win nor did he collect his winnings. He waited until six months after the divorce was final. By that time, he had made arrangements to live in Peru and have his annual $120,000 installment check sent to him there. Guess what? His now former wife found out about the win and sued him for half the winnings claiming they were won while they were still legally married and thus belonged to both of them.

When the case finally came to court the judge ruled that Dr. Giha did not have to share his winnings, even though he won them before their divorce was final. The judge said, "The fact that he won $2.4 million was most fortuitous. But what if he had lost $2.4 million? Could he have returned to the court and requested that Mrs. Giha share in his debt?" Not likely. Dr. Giha got to keep it all.

But at least one state has ruled differently on this issue. Maryland's Court of Special Appeals has ruled that a Maryland man who won a $1 million D.C. Lotto grand prize had to share half his winnings with his ex-wife because the divorce was not final when the husband won the prize. The former husband and wife will split the remaining 18 years of annual $35,000 payments 50-50.

What happens if we file for bankruptcy and then win the lottery?

Q: My wife and I have been having considerable financial difficulty for the last couple of years and recently have had to file for bankruptcy. In the meantime, we still buy a couple of lottery tickets each week dreaming that we'll win and be able to get back on our feet. But what would happen if we did win this week? Would we be able to keep our winnings, or would the winnings be turned over to creditors?

A: Any lottery winnings you receive after you have filed for bankruptcy cannot be touched by creditors. If creditors could take your money after you filed, that would defeat the whole purpose of the protection given you by the bankruptcy court. Bankruptcy proceedings are designed to give you a fresh start. Good luck.

Incidentally, it has happened that recently bankrupt people have won lottery jackpots. On August 14, 1990, Frank and Constance Drigotas of Maine filed for bankruptcy. About six weeks later the Drigotas won a $1.1 million Tri-State Megabucks jackpot.

Can a winner's future lottery payments be reduced for any reason?

Q: If a person wins a lottery jackpot and begins receiving the annual payments, can the lottery reduce the amount of future payments for any reason? What if the economy gets really bad or the state lottery loses money, could a winner receive less than promised?

A: No, the lottery will never give winners less than they have won, no matter what happens to the economy or to the lottery itself. The money that is used to pay winners is invested in long-term investments that are absolutely guaranteed by both the financial institution which has the money in a trust and by the state itself. Rest assured that if you win the lottery, you will receive every cent coming to you.

A couple of things can go wrong, however, and can reduce the amount of money that a winner receives in future years, but they have nothing to do with the lottery itself. Sometimes the IRS raises the amount of taxes it deducts from winnings, or steps in and claims future payments in order to clear up past due amounts owed the government, and sometimes lawsuits will strip a lottery winner of some or all of future payments.

Take, for example, the case of Sylvia Trapuzzano who won $8.25 million in the Pennsylvania Lottery in April, 1989. In December 1991, after receiving three annual payments, a Pennsylvania court ruled that Trapuzzano had to share half of her winnings with her former live-in boyfriend, Gary Fender. Fender claimed that Trapuzzano had promised him half of her jackpot, and the court agreed. The court ordered Trapuzzano to pay Fender half of the $952,574 she had already received and ordered the Pennsylvania Lottery to divide future payments between Trapuzzano and Fender.

How come Indian reservations can offer a lottery separate from the state lottery?

Q: My friend from Wisconsin says that the Indian reservation near his home conducts a lottery that is separate from the state lottery, and that the odds are better than the state's lottery odds. How is it possible to have a lottery within a lottery state, but not associated with the state lottery? Wouldn't these two lotteries compete with one another?

A: Your friend is probably talking about the lottery run by the Oneida Tribe from their reservation, about seven miles west of Green Bay. Federal law permits Indian tribes to operate various forms of gambling such as bingo, casino games, and lotteries independently of the state in which the tribe is located.

The Oneida lottery, called The Big Green, began in April of 1988, and it offers better odds but smaller jackpots than the Wisconsin Lotto. The lottery is strictly run by the tribe, and the Wisconsin Lottery has no say in matters. In fact, the Oneida Tribe is able to sell subscriptions for The Big Green to out-of-state residents, something that is prohibited by the Wisconsin Lottery, as well as every other lottery state.

The proceeds of the reservation's lottery and the highly successful bingo games benefit the Oneida Tribe. The money is deposited into a general fund and distributed into nearly 60 programs, including education, health care and social services on the reservation.

Why don't we ever hear the results of bonus drawings?

Q: Could you tell us why we never hear the results of any bonus drawings that our state lotteries conduct? There is never anything in the newspapers about when the drawings are or who, if anyone, wins. I always send in my losing tickets for these drawings and then get frustrated because I never even hear if the drawings take place.

A: All those bonus and second chance drawings do take place and people do win, but there is little public notice. The lottery routinely sends out press releases identifying drawings and winners—I know because I receive them—but newspapers and other news media seldom print that information or inform the public in any way. These "minor" lottery events have become old hat, not of any great interest to newspaper readers, radio listeners or TV viewers.

Rest assured that if you had been selected as a "bonus" participant or if you had won anything, you would have been contacted by the lottery. Since you haven't heard anything, like most of us, you haven't been lucky yet.

PART V

This Actually Happened!

It's true! A California woman sued the state of California when she didn't win the big prize—and she won the lawsuit and $3 million. Hmmmm. That gives me an idea.

Is there a "lottery tickets for guns" swap taking place?

Q: Is it true that some lottery has a "Lottery Tickets for Guns" swap program? How does it work, and has anyone turned in a gun for lottery tickets? I'd like to find out how to do the same thing in our community.

A: More than one community has implemented this idea. The Scituate, Rhode Island, Police Department was the first organization that I heard of that exchanged lottery tickets for guns in 1993. Then, in late February 1994 in Iowa, more than 1,000 guns were turned in during just one weekend in the cities of Dubuque, Cedar Rapids, Waterloo, and Iowa City in exchange for lottery tickets. Individuals who turned in guns were given 25 lottery tickets and a $25 food certificate from Handi-Mart Food Stores. The program was initiated by KGAN-TV in Cedar Rapids but supported by the Iowa State Lottery. The Iowa Lottery provided the lottery tickets and HandiMart Food Stores contributed the food certificates.

One lottery-related organization that is encouraging the idea of lottery-tickets-for-guns programs is *LottoWorld* magazine. *LottoWorld,* under the direction of Editor-in-Chief Rich Holman, has put together a position paper regarding implementing similar programs in other communities. If you would like to receive a copy of this six-page "Guns for Lottery Tickets" program, send a self-addressed and stamped (87 cents) envelope to Rich Holman, *LottoWorld,* 2150 Goodlette Road, Suite 200, Naples, FL 33940, and ask for it.

Is selling interstate lottery tickets against the law?

Q: What's all this fuss I've been reading about where police are raiding lottery ticket sellers who sell out-of-state lottery tickets and closing them down? I don't understand. What's illegal about selling lottery tickets for one state to residents of another state? We don't have any restrictions like this on anything else. Why lottery tickets?

A: You are referring to an ongoing controversy in lottery ticket selling. Several states have passed legislation making it illegal to sell their lottery tickets outside of their states. This has even resulted in some arrests. In January 1994, police in Monticello, Illinois, arrested Phillip Gillespie, president of U.S. Lottery Group, and raided U.S. Lottery Group's offices claiming the organization was selling illegal lottery tickets. U.S. Lottery Group is a lottery tickets "subscription service" that specializes in purchasing out-of-state lottery tickets for its customers and reselling them at an increased price. U.S. Lottery Group has been doing this for 15 years.

At the same time that Gillespie was arrested, Texas Lottery officials and Texas police stopped U.S. Lottery Group's Texas representatives from buying Texas Lottery tickets for out-of-state players who had contracted with U.S. Lottery Group in Illinois to purchase the Texas lottery tickets.

The two Texas representatives of U.S. Lottery Group, Bonnie and Sol Strickland, were surprised by all the commotion. They had been buying from 500 to 5000 Texas Lottery tickets for U.S. Lottery Group every week—and at the same store—since shortly after Texas started selling lotto tickets.

U.S. Lottery Group in Illinois would take the orders for the $1 Texas Lotto tickets by telephone from people all over the country, charging the customers $2 for each ticket ordered, and then would hire the Stricklands to do the actual purchasing of the tickets in Texas.

The problem is that Texas law makes it illegal to sell Texas lottery tickets without a license issued by the Texas Lottery, and it's illegal to charge more than face value ($1) for them. Many states ban resale of lottery tickets, and Texas officials boast that their state's law is among the toughest.

In the last few years, not only have there been several legal challenges of a state's right to restrict out-of-state reselling of lottery tickets, but additionally, there has been federal legislation proposed that would make it illegal to sell out-of-state lottery tickets in any state. At this writing, Senator Arlen Specter of Pennsylvania has proposed an amendment to the anti-crime bill to make it illegal to sell out-of-state lottery tickets any place in the country.

However, at least one well-organized lobbying organization that I know of (because they have a mailing list of "influential pro-lottery celebrities" with my name on it) is fighting hard to keep this amendment from being included in the anti-crime bill. The organization, C.H.A.N.C.E. (Coalition to Halt Anti-Lottery Nonsense and for Commercial Enterprise), has sent pre-addressed letters and envelopes to lottery players nationwide inviting them to sign and mail these anti-amendment letters back to their representatives in the House of Representatives.

Since the matter is still undecided, most subscription companies selling lottery tickets are still buying out-of-state tickets as usual for their customers, waiting for Congress and the courts to make some more decisions.

How can you mark millions of play slips quickly?

Q: I hear that some group has figured out how to get around the problem of marking the millions of play slips necessary to purchase all the possible number combinations for a large lotto jackpot and thereby can guarantee a win. Have you heard anything about this? How can this be done?

A: The Australian International Lotto Fund used computers and electronic printers to mark play slips when they bought more than five million of the seven million lotto tickets for the February 15, 1992, drawing and won the $27 million jackpot. By using the computer-connected electronic printers, the group was able to print individual play slips with non-repeating number combinations much faster than if they had been filled out by hand. Several other groups since then have indicated that they will do the same thing for other state lotteries that offer giant jackpots. But it probably won't help them win.

State lottery commissions moved quickly to block huge purchases of tickets that enable groups to buy every number combination for a drawing. The Virginia Lottery Board, for example, reacting to the February 15, 1992, win, approved an emergency regulation that prohibits the use of play slips that have not been *manually* marked.

The regulation, passed at the May 20, 1992, Lottery Board meeting and signed into effect immediately by the governor, reads:

". . . If a play slip is used to select the player's number or numbers for an on-line game, the play slip number selections shall be manually marked and not marked by any electro-mechanical, electronic printing or other automated device. Any play slip marked by methods other than those authorized by these regulations is invalid and subject to seizure by the department if presented for play at any lottery terminal. Any tickets produced from the use of invalid play slips are also invalid and subject to seizure by the department."

All state lotteries are adding new regulations that will prohibit groups from purchasing all the possible number combinations for a drawing and thereby guarantee a win. The purpose of these regulations is to put all players on the same footing for each drawing.

Who owns the "mistake" ticket?

Q: I work in a convenience store that sells lottery tickets. Occasionally a clerk will make a mistake and print out a ticket that the customer doesn't want. We always try to sell any "mistakes" to customers, but if we don't, the store owner has to pay for the

ticket. The few times that this has happened the owner hasn't won anything with these "mistake" tickets, although all of us (especially the clerk who was responsible for the "mistake") will be delighted if he does win something. That's why I was glad to read in your column that the clerk in South Dakota who cashed in the winning $12 million "mistake" lotto ticket that she found lying on the cash register was forced to share the jackpot with the store owner. My fellow workers and I believe, however, that the owner should have gotten it all.

A: Although the South Dakota clerk you are referring to bought the "mistake" ticket, that ticket had been lying around for a few days and she only bought it after she discovered it was the winning ticket. In similar cases, courts have been saying that "mistakes" belong to the store owner, not the clerks.

In a somewhat related case, employees of a Washington convenience store bought a lotto ticket and paid for it with money from a cup in which customers left unwanted small change when they made their purchases. That ticket won $4 million. The store owner sued for ownership of the ticket, saying that the money used to buy the ticket belonged to him as the store owner. The court agreed. However, the judge said, the owner had clearly indicated that employees would share proceeds of any winning lottery ticket. As a result, the 10 store employees and the owner shared the winnings.

Do state lotteries contribute to compulsive gambling?

Q: What's your opinion about whether or not state lotteries contribute to the problem of compulsive gambling? I believe I read somewhere that all state lotteries are now setting up toll-free "hotline" telephone numbers for people with compulsive gambling problems caused by the playing of lotteries.

A: First of all, not all states are setting up compulsive gambling "hotlines" and they are not exclusively for lottery players. They are hotlines for compulsive gamblers of any sort. The lottery is just promoting the program and footing the bill. Only a few states, such as the District of Columbia, Florida, Maryland, Minnesota, New Jersey, and Ohio, have started, or are considering instituting, these programs. New Jersey has even gone so far as to have the following message printed on the back of all lottery tickets and on decals placed on all 5000 computerized lottery sales terminals throughout the state: "If you or someone you know has a gambling problem, call: 1-800-GAMBLER."

What do I think of these programs? I think they are fine. They can't hurt callers and they certainly hold the possibility of providing help for compulsive gamblers who may call them. But, for a different reason, they make me a bit uncomfortable.

Unfortunately, these programs have been associated with lottery playing because politicians or lottery officials for reasons of politics and public relations want to give the impression that their lottery is socially responsible. The problem is that as more and more exposure is given to these "lottery" compulsive gambling hotlines, the public is likely to begin associating lottery playing with compulsive gambling, and there may be an anti-lottery backlash. The public may start asking why there should even be a lottery if it does bad things. See the problem?

And one more thing. We hear a lot about these few lottery sponsored "hotlines" for compulsive gamblers being set up, but we never hear anything about them after it is announced that they are being set up. Does anyone call? More importantly, do compulsive lottery players call? In fact, are there many (any?) compulsive lottery players around? State lotteries would be wise to let the public know what's happening with these programs.

Why don't "big spin" players form a pool and all win?

Q: Our state lottery has periodic drawings in which several people who have sent in ENTRY tickets get those tickets drawn somehow and then are invited to a special "big spin" contest. Each of the contestants gets a chance to spin a big roulette-type wheel and win up to a million dollars. Each person wins something, at least $10,000. That gives me a great idea. Why don't the several contestants get together before the spinning and form a pool? This pool would be guaranteed to win! They could agree to pool their winnings and then split those winnings equally after the contest. After all, it is likely that some contestants will win small while others will win big and this way even the small winners will receive more from the big winners. The only people who might not like this are the people who win big. But then again, no one knows who is going to be a big winner. What do you think?

A: I like it, and it has been done many times. Lottery "spin" players are figuring out how to maximize their chances at winning big dollars on these lottery last-chance contests and this is by far the best way. For example, in February of last year, 62-year-old Mabel Long and six other players had their ENTRY tickets drawn by the Florida Lottery for the Cool Million game. Shortly before the game began, the contestants agreed to pool their winnings and split the pot equally. While Mabel eventually won the $1 million, she had no hesitation about adding it to the pool as agreed. "We were all in need," she said, "We didn't know which one would come out on top and which one would come out on the bottom," Consequently, each of the contestants took home $129,000 after taxes. When it comes to lotteries, pools are usually a great idea.

Can you sue the lottery when you don't win?

Q: I heard that a California woman sued the state of California when she didn't win the big prize—and she won the law-

suit and $3 million. I lose all the time. It sounds like it might pay to sue. What are the details?

A: You are referring to Doris Barnett, one of the contestants on California's Big Spin television show on Dec. 30, 1985. She spun the wheel and the ball landed in the slot signaling a $3 million win. Geoff Edwards, the Big Spin host, excitedly declared her the grand prize winner.

Hooray!

But within seconds, and while Doris Barnett and her family excitedly were congratulating each other and being applauded by Edwards and the studio audience, the ball popped out and dropped into the $10,000 slot, where it stayed.

Immediately, Lottery officials on the scene made the decision that the ball had not remained in the $3 million slot the required five seconds before it fell into the $10,000 slot. They further declared that host Edwards had made a mistake and was premature in announcing the Grand Prize Win.

Winner Barnett sued—and didn't cash the $10,000 check.

A Los Angeles Superior Court jury, after hearing both sides of the issue and viewing several tapes of the drawing, made its decision. The jurors not only decided that the $3 million prize belonged to Barnett but also awarded her $400,000 extra in damages for the emotional trauma she suffered when the prize was taken away.

In a different lawsuit that hasn't been decided yet, Frances Bobnar, a 32-year-old single mother living in Adamsbury, Pennsylvania, says she is suing the Pennsylvania Lottery Commission for $1.5 million because she "never wins" and the Pennsylvania Lottery says "if you play, you win." One of the Pennsylvania Lottery slogans is "You've got to play to win." Bobnar claims that she, family members and friends have bought about $150,000 in tickets over the past 10 years. Bobnar, who expects another child in several months, says she has been plagued with legal fees, has a paternity suit pending and lives on public assistance, and this lawsuit may change all that.

It could take several years before Bobnar's case comes up, yet she is patient. She believes the $100 she spent so far to file the lawsuit is "money well spent." The Pennsylvania Lottery Commission doesn't seem too nervous about this lawsuit.

Why is a winner suing the lottery ticket seller who sold her the winning ticket?

Q: Do you know anything about a woman in Illinois who is suing the lottery ticket seller where she bought her winning jackpot ticket? Apparently she is suing because they are keeping her from collecting all of her money. What's going on here?

A: You are referring to the case in which an Illinois Little Lotto millionaire wants to be a big lotto millionaire.

Carol Stonecipher, 41, of Elburn, Illinois, was elated when she saw in early August that she had correctly picked the winning numbers for the $11 million Illinois Lotto. She had purchased her winning ticket at the Pride Pantry store in the Chicago suburb of Maple Park shortly before the drawing that night. However, her elation was short-lived when she found out there were five other winning tickets. That meant that instead of winning $11 million dollars, she would receive only about $1.8 million. This is a difference between receiving $379,500 every year after taxes for 20 years, or receiving $62,250 annually. But to make this even worse, it turns out that all five of the other winning tickets were held by the clerk at the Pride Pantry store where she had purchased her winning ticket.

It appears that the clerk hadn't intended to print out the additional winning tickets but the machine had momentarily jammed and the clerk, in an apparent attempt to resolve the problem began pressing various keys on the terminal. At that point, six tickets were printed. The clerk had put the unwanted tickets in the drawer and on Sunday, August 1, 1993, a store employee realized that those tickets were five-sixths of the total lottery prize.

Within a matter of days, there were three parties laying claim to all or part of the jackpot: Stonecipher was claiming all of the prize, the store's owners were claiming five-sixths for the five duplicate tickets, and the clerk was claiming the same five-sixths. According to Stonecipher, the clerk led her to believe that he was going to void the duplicate tickets. However, the clerk is claiming that he did indeed buy the duplicate tickets from the store as he would be permitted to do under Illinois law.

This is an extremely interesting case because the store or clerk had to pay for the tickets since they were printed and numbers were recorded by the Illinois Lottery, mistake or no mistake. As lottery players, we know there are no guarantees regarding multiple winning tickets! On the other hand, a retailer's mistake did cost Carol millions. We have yet to see how this will turn out.

This case is another good example of my theory that the best way to win a lottery jackpot is to keep any "mistakes" issued to you. Those tickets issued by mistake always seem to win.

Which lottery gave free lottery tickets to pet owners?

Q: I heard that some state lottery is giving free lottery tickets to pet owners. What's that all about, and what lottery is doing it? With all the pets we have we could earn lots of tickets.

A: The West Virginia Lottery launched a program to encourage pet owners to neuter or spay their dogs and cats. The lottery offered 20 lottery tickets to anyone who adopted a pet at animal shelters in a select number of counties and proved that a veterinarian had spayed or neutered the animal.

Additionally, the lottery offered anyone donating at least $3 in dog or cat food to shelters in these same counties a coupon for five instant lottery tickets.

The West Virginia Lottery reports that public response to the offer of free tickets was overwhelming.

Do the number picking machines ever get jammed?

Q: Do the lottery number picking machines ever mess up and refuse to work? I watch the drawings frequently and although I have never seen the machines malfunction, I keep hoping that they will so that I can see how the hostess—who is always so cool, efficient and professional—will handle things. Actually, I guess I'd like to see some excitement added to the drawings, especially since I never seem to have any winning numbers.

A: I am sorry, but you probably aren't going to see any state lottery hostess shriek in dismay or burst into tears if a drawing machine malfunctions. Since each drawing is live, each hostess is trained to handle potential machine malfunctions in that same cool, professional way you are used to seeing at each drawing.

Drawing machine malfunctions do occur, however. The most recent one that I know of occurred in Delaware. On WHYY-TV, shortly after the drawing started, a door on the drawing machine popped open and the first two balls fell out onto the floor. A third ball, number 36, stayed in the machine when the drawing hostess hurriedly reclosed the door. The drawing manager who was standing by, stopped the drawing, declaring it a misdraw, and after checking the equipment, drew five additional balls off camera to complete the drawing. Because the number 36 ball stayed in the chute, it was included as one of the official winning numbers. The two balls that dropped on the floor were not included in the winning numbers. New drawing machines have been ordered.

Should I save my non-winning lottery tickets?

Q: Other than for tax purposes, is there any reason to save non-winning lottery tickets when they are not scratch-off tickets? I know that sometimes non-winning instant game tickets may be sent in to the lottery to be entered in special "losers' drawings," but I don't think there has ever been a drawing in our state for losing pick-3, pick-4, or lotto tickets.

A: In past years, lotteries attempted to promote the purchase of their instant game tickets by allowing players to send in only scratch-off tickets to "Loser's Lottery" drawings, but that seems to be changing. Now it appears that some states are rethinking that policy and are beginning to offer second-chance drawings that allow players to send in losing tickets from different lottery games.

The West Virginia Lottery, for example, has asked players to mail in non-winning tickets from their daily 3, daily 4, and daily 5 games, and from lotto. Each envelope sent in that contained one ticket from each of the games was entered in a special drawing in which the prizes ranged from $2,000 to $50,000. The idea behind this promotion was the cross-merchandising of all the games that the West Virginia Lottery offers.

This type of cross-merchandising of all games is becoming common with lotteries, so you should probably save your losing lottery tickets of all types in anticipation of similar second-chance drawings being conducted in the future by your state lottery.

What store hides lottery tickets in groceries?

Q: I heard a brief mention on the news the other night that some grocery store owner someplace is hiding instant lottery tickets in groceries and that when people get home and open their packages of food, they find these free lottery tickets. What store is this?

A: I don't know which store you heard about because many smaller, non-chain stores do this (larger, chain supermarkets do not do this) in every lottery state as a good way to create customer interest and to move some of the older instant game tickets that aren't selling as well. It seems to work well and customers enjoy the thrill of discovering the scratch-off tickets in their groceries.

One store owner that I know of, Rusty Hiltunen of Rusty's Food Land in Howard, South Dakota, has been hiding instant game tickets (wrapped in plastic bags) in random packages of fresh meat. He has been giving away about 30 instant game tickets a month this way since he started selling lottery tickets and plans to continue doing so. He says that his customers love it and brag to one another about finding a lottery ticket in their groceries.

Are simultaneous big jackpots planned by different states?

Q: Why is it that whenever there is a large jackpot in our state it seems that several other states have giant jackpots also? Is there some inter-lottery planning going on?

A: Many states have lottery drawings on the same day each week, so it is likely that there will be other big jackpots on the same date. Although the national publicity created by a large jackpot in one state may spur residents in other states to play their own games, don't read any more into it than it deserves. It is pure coincidence.

What happened to the lottery funds collected by the state?

Q: I would like to know specifically—and in detail—how the lottery funds that our state collected in the last 12 months were actually spent. I know that at least a portion of those funds were supposed to go to local schools and colleges, but I have not heard if any of these funds really do get to schools. In fact, I have heard many rumors to the contrary. I am especially curious as to how much our local school district received as its share of lottery funds and how those funds were spent. What was purchased? Is there any way I can find this out?

A: Yes, all you have to do is ask. Every state lottery goes out of its way to be financially accountable to its players and to its state citizenry. Usually this accountability takes the form of an annual report that tells how much money was received by the lottery, how much was paid out in prizes, how much was spent for administration, advertising, and paying lottery ticket retailers, and how much the state kept for its projects. It's these state "projects" that you will want to find out about.

Usually each state lottery issues a second report each year that identifies how much of this money that was received by the state was actually spent for different projects. You can receive a copy of the lottery annual report and a copy of lottery project expenditures simply by contacting the lottery and requesting this information. A good place to start is by calling the lottery toll-free number and asking to be directed to the person who will send you this information. The lottery will send the information to you by return mail. It would be too expensive to send these reports to everyone in the state each year, so state lotteries wait for interested people to request the information. Surprisingly, not very many people are actually interested.

In the case of lottery money designated for education, funds are divided up among the state's school districts according to student population. The lottery requires that school districts report back to them how the money is spent. The lottery then compiles this information and has it ready for people like you when you ask.

For example, I recently received the annual report of expenditures from the Idaho Lottery. Idaho designates its lottery funds for "public schools and buildings." In this hot pink brochure entitled "Where the Money Goes," every school district is identified, along with how much money it received in the past year, what it was spent for, and how much the district has received since inception of the Idaho Lottery.

What was purchased? Along with many purchases of school buses, roof repairs, building remodeling, and equipment replacement, districts bought such things as new bleachers, heating systems, portable classrooms, telephone system upgrades, an all-weather track, 20 acres of land for future building projects, asbestos removal, underground sprinkler installation, water line installation, sewer drainfield repairs, and a cafeteria stove upgrade.

Which lottery gives players a chance to design an instant game?

Q: I understand that some state lottery sponsors a contest to give players a chance to design a scratch-off game. I'd love to know more about this. I've wanted to suggest a couple of instant game designs that I have come up with, but I haven't known how to do it. Perhaps this is the way I can get my foot in the door. Actually, what I'd really like to do is design instant games for a living. I've got dozens of game ideas in my head and on paper. Any information about which state lottery is having this contest would be appreciated.

A: This may still be your big chance. But it appears that you are not the only player to dream about creating your own instant game—one that you just know will be a big hit with other lottery players. It seems that there are thousands of you. The

Oregon Lottery recognized this and decided to capitalize on this interest to help promote a brand new scratch-off product line this past fall. Since October 1993, Oregon instant tickets have had higher payouts, which means more prize money and higher average prizes, and there is a greater variety of games than ever before—including six designs during 1994 created by players.

Players were encouraged to enter the "Designer Scratch-it Contest" by requesting an official entry form from the Oregon Lottery. Lottery officials say that designs were judged on whether they were in keeping with the Oregon Lottery's image of "good taste and fairness." Anyone could enter the contest. You didn't need to be an artist; you just had to be creative and original and show the lottery what you thought a scratch-off ticket should be. Entries were judged on game theme, play style, originality, graphics, and appropriateness. Oh yes. What did designers win? The best design won $5,000. Five runners-up received prizes of $1,000 each. All six games selected will be produced and join a long list of successful Oregon Lottery scratch-off games.

Even though you missed this first competition, look for it to be repeated every year.

Is there a watch that picks winning numbers?

Q: What's this I hear about some lottery player who has a watch that not only picks winning lottery numbers but also somehow notifies him of the winning numbers when they are drawn by the lottery? Is such a thing possible? A Dick Tracy lottery watch?

A: Some people check their wrist watches to learn the time, or possibly the date, but Oregon Lottery player Thomas Cordrey learned much bigger news from his timepiece. It seems that Tom, 52, held the single winning ticket for a $7 million jackpot. Tom had used quick pick—not his watch—to select his numbers but did use the watch to find out the winning numbers.

It seems that Tom owns something called a receptor watch which somehow picks up information through radio wave transmissions. Tom says that he not only picks up the weather reports on his watch, he also can pick up lottery numbers. He checked his watch right after the drawing and says, "I saw all my numbers there." I'm still trying to find out how these watches work and where they are sold.

Tom elected to receive a lump-sum payment of $3.5 million. After 28% was withheld for federal taxes, Tom left lottery head-quarters with a check for $2,520,000.

What happened last year?

Q: Usually some pretty bizarre stuff happens in the lottery each year. What were the "highlights" of the past year?

A: All kinds of great stuff happened with lotteries last year. Here it is: The 1993 "Lottery Highlights of the Year."

Not so bizarre is the fact that Nebraska and Georgia became the 36th and 37th U.S. Lotteries during the year. Within a few years, all states will have lotteries.

The federal income tax that is automatically deducted from large lottery wins was increased from 20 to 28%. The IRS said that this would keep lottery winners from having to pay so much extra when they filed annual tax forms at the end of the year.

Powerball grabbed the limelight this year by awarding a $111 million jackpot to one person, Leslie Robbins, an English teacher in Fond du Lac, Wisconsin, who claimed the prize in partnership with his fiancée. This couple will now receive about $3.6 million a year for the next 20 years. However, the real highlight of this story was Robbins' claim that he was going to keep his $30,000-a-year teaching job. He did—for half the year—and then took a leave of absence, assuring the media that he would be back next year. What do you want to bet he doesn't return to the classroom next year?

Incidentally, Robbins purchased the $111 million ticket along a stretch of road known locally as "Miracle Mile" because three winning multi-million-dollar lottery tickets have been purchased there by players in the last three years.

If you think returning to a teaching job after becoming a millionaire is crazy, how about $5.9 million lottery winner Albert Knights? He also returned to his job, even though his wife tried to talk him into retiring, arguing that the $190,000 a year they were going to receive for the next 20 years was more than enough to take care of their needs. Albert wouldn't hear of retiring, however. Besides, he liked his job as driver of a garbage truck.

"Loser of the Year" is undoubtedly Carol Stonecipher—who was also a winner. On July 31, as you read a few pages back, a lottery computer turned out six identical tickets because of computer delay and human error, when Carol wanted only one for the $11 million Illinois Lotto jackpot. Allegedly, the extra six tickets were to be canceled, but they weren't. Sure enough, those numbers won. Now Carol, who consequently only won one-sixth of the jackpot, is in court fighting for the rights to those other five tickets and the other five-sixths of the jackpot. The clerk and the store owner are also battling for ownership of the five "mistake" tickets.

"Winner of the Year" has to be one of two guys. One man found $10 in the parking lot of a store and figured it was his lucky day. He took the $10 into the store and bought lottery tickets with it. It turns out that one of the tickets was worth over a million dollars. Another man in Ohio accidentally left his winning lotto ticket in his pocket and it was destroyed in the wash. However, after he provided evidence that the winning ticket was in the middle of a sequence of tickets he bought, the Ohio House and Senate passed a special legislation that named him the winner and he became a lotto millionaire without turning in a winning ticket. That *never* happens.

But my favorite bizarre lottery story for 1993 has to be about

Enrique Mendes, who decided to teach his lottery-fanatic wife a lesson by playing a bit of a prank on her. I'm not even certain that this story is true. My "sources" assure me that it is. It seems that Mendes' wife had just spent her entire paycheck on lottery tickets. According to the *Weekly World News,* Mendes constructed a bogus lottery ticket that made her think she had won $45 million. When he gave her the ticket she began shaking and screaming: "I won! I won!" Unfortunately, she then clutched her chest, made a gasping noise, fell on the floor, and died. Mendes said, "My only consolation is knowing that she died happy." At least that is what the *Weekly World News* reported.

Have any ideas for a lottery license plate?

Q: I think I saw a lottery license plate the other day. A Florida license plate on a passing car read, FL LOTTO. Have you seen any lottery license plates? In my state we can purchase special "vanity" license plates for an additional $10, and I'm thinking of getting one. My only problem is I don't know what to say on the plate. Any ideas?

A: I have seen only one lottery-related license plate and it was on a rather impressive-looking Italian sports car. Like the one you saw, it read, CA LOTTO.

Perhaps these lottery license plates that other readers have told me about may suggest possibilities for you: 1 LOTTO, QUIK PIK, EASY PIK, FANTAC5 (Fantasy Five), LOT WINR, I15G VL (I won $5000, Virginia Lottery), LKY NMBR.

Have fun. Spend an evening dreaming up your lottery plates.

Where can I design a lottery billboard?

Q: Do you know anything about a state lottery that is having a contest to see who can design a lottery billboard? It sounds like a contest made for me. Any information would be helpful.

A: You are talking about the California Lottery's SuperLotto Billboard contest. Unfortunately, you are too late. It's already over. But maybe it'll happen again.

The billboard contest that challenged players to "design a better billboard than our ad agency" had two purposes: to create awareness of California's new SuperLotto game and also to give players the chance to have direct input into the advertising for the new game. And it worked. Well over 2500 ideas were submitted.

The first place winning idea (submitted by Eric Smith of San Diego) features the image of George Washington (the same picture of George that is on the $1 bill) staring at the jackpot amount. Underneath is the slogan, "I'd buy that for a dollar."

The second place winning idea was submitted by Scott Clark of El Segundo. He showed a driver's view of a mountain scene with the slogan underneath that reads, "Permanent Vacation Ahead."

Third place was won by Kurt Lighthouse of San Francisco. His winning idea featured the slogan, "Run away and buy a circus." I like that one.

Which lottery gave away football bowl tickets?

Q: Which lottery gives away football bowl tickets? That's a good prize. I wish our lottery would do the same thing.

A: Several state lotteries give away football tickets as prizes in order to promote specific lottery games. Frequently, state lotteries give away football game tickets for bowl games—but usually only when one of the teams playing is from the lottery state.

For example, the Oregon Lottery gave away 50 trips for two

to Oregon Keno game winners so that they could go cheer the University of Oregon Ducks in the Independence Bowl in 1992 when they played Wake Forest in Shreveport, Louisiana. The prize package included air transportation, accommodations for two nights, and tickets to the bowl game.

When do jackpot winners receive their second and subsequent checks?

Q: I understand that when you win a large lottery jackpot that has to be paid to you over a number of years, you receive your first year's check within a few days after turning in your winning ticket to the lottery. But when do you receive your second and subsequent checks? Is your second check received one year after the drawing of the winning numbers or a year from the date that you received your first check? It makes a difference because sometimes there is a significant delay between the date of the drawing and the date that the winning ticket is turned in. Also, sometimes several different people win the same jackpot and share the winnings. Even though they turn in their winning tickets at different times, are they all paid on the same date the next year?

A: Winners are paid second-year and subsequent-year payments differently in different states. The most frequent method of payment used by lotteries is to set up four days in the year, each three months apart, when winners can collect their annual payments. Winners receive their payments on the earliest date following the date on which they won their prizes. Winners may collect their annual winnings in person or have checks mailed to them or directly to their banks.

Does anyone actually win the instant game "big" prizes?

Q: I enjoy playing our Lottery's different scratch-off instant games and quite often I win small amounts of money. I am convinced that the instant games are the games to play if you enjoy winning. However, even though each scratch-off game offers chances to win larger prizes, sometimes $1,000, $5,000, or even $25,000, I never hear of anyone actually winning them, and I certainly never have myself. I guess I'd like your reassurance that those "big" prizes really are going to instant game players.

A: Rest assured that thousands of players just like you are winning the "big" instant game prizes. I receive press releases daily from every state lottery, often with pictures, telling about instant-game winners of sizable amounts. Unfortunately, compared to lotto winners these instant-game winners are considered "small" winners by the news media and don't get interviewed in the newspapers or on the six o'clock news.

You might enjoy hearing about the amazing luck of a fellow instant-game player. In 1991, Frank Brooks of Virginia bought several instant-game tickets and scratched them off. One of his tickets was a $10,000 winner. Less than three weeks later, an instant-game ticket which he purchased at the same store and for the same instant game turned out to be a $20,000 winner. Brooks' total of 34 tickets yielded him $30,000!

What are the chances of that happening to you? The chances of getting a $10,000 winning ticket in the game he was playing are 1 in 480,000, and 1 in 1.4 million for a $20,000 winner. Buying only 34 tickets made the chances of winning both prizes in that game well over 1 in 19 billion. Billion, not million.

Why can't I get through on our toll-free lottery player information line?

Q: I have tried calling our state's toll-free player information line following the lotto drawing on dozens of occasions, but I can never get through. All I get is a busy signal. What's the problem?

A: You are calling at the wrong time. The worst time to call is each night after the pick-3, pick-4, pick-5, or lotto drawings. That's when everyone is trying to get through, 95% of the lines are being used and you are likely to get a busy signal.

Lottery officials suggest that you try waiting at least a couple of hours after the drawings before you call—if you can wait that long. Mornings are an even better time to call.

Why do all winners come from the same small geographical area?

Q: I live in the Dallas-Ft. Worth region in Texas and play the Texas Lottery on a regular basis. As you know, we have a very active lottery state and a lot of million-dollar jackpots. The problem is, it seems that the winners all come from one very small area of Texas, and not many from around here. What's going on?

A: Probably nothing sinister, if that's what you are implying—it's just the luck of the draw. If, however, this same area continues to monopolize the majority of winners over the next several months, even I will be questioning what is going on in Texas.

The area of Texas that seems to have the corner on lottery winners recently, is Corpus Christi. In July 1993, this area produced four millionaires in four drawings. It is highly unusual that one area of a state, especially a relatively small area, could have such a run of good luck, but it does happen. For example, there is a one-mile stretch of South Main Street in Fond Du Lac, Wisconsin, that has also had an incredible run of good luck. This one-mile stretch has previously had lottery players win $20 million in the spring of 1990 and $21 million in the summer of 1990. Then on August 6, 1993, Leslie Robbins and his fiancée, Colleen DeVries, a couple who lived in a 520-square-foot apartment on that stretch of road, won the richest single winning ticket in U.S. lottery history. Their Powerball ticket was worth more than $111 million, the third largest jackpot in the U.S. It almost makes you want to move to this "Miracle Mile."

Are lotteries using recyclable, biodegradable paper for tickets?

Q: At least two years ago I read that state lotteries were developing an environmentally friendly ticket stock for their instant games that would continue to assure security for the lottery but would also allow scratch-off tickets to be recycled. Apparently instant tickets are made with bits of metal and other substances that prohibit them from being recycled like other paper products. Has it happened yet? Have state lotteries figured out how to use recyclable, biodegradable paper stock?

A: Yes. Several lotteries have already switched to printing their instant-game tickets on "friendly" paper. You are not the only person concerned about state lotteries printing their instant tickets on non-recyclable paper. One lottery official I spoke with said that he hoped that environmentalist groups don't discover just how many millions of foil-filled instant tickets are being discarded in lottery states every month. It is every lottery's worst nightmare to contemplate an organized environmentalist protest or boycott aimed at their instant games.

Up until now the lottery industry has used foil-enriched paper for instant tickets for security reasons. A foil ticket is less susceptible to tampering and forgery because of its composition and because it uses high-tech color printers. In addition, a foil ticket is generally more attractive than a plain paper ticket.

But that is changing. The Ohio Lottery is currently selling a recyclable instant ticket in a test to determine the viability of non-foil tickets. If there are no problems discovered, these "green" tickets will be used statewide, with other lottery states following suit soon after. A special black and white security paper made in Sweden is being used in this Ohio test. Not only is this paper foil-free and recyclable, its unique properties make cut-and-paste forgeries impossible.

The Minnesota Lottery has also announced that it has started printing instant-game tickets on new ticket stock. This new paper stock is called TERRA 2000 and enables the lottery to print tickets on plain, biodegradable paper while maintaining the high level of security required by lotteries throughout the world. The printing of lottery tickets, especially instant tickets, is treated like the government treats the printing of money. A special paper stock, with a composition not easily duplicated by counterfeiters, must be used to keep unscrupulous people from easily printing up their own instant winners. Until recently, attempts at developing a ticket stock that afforded a high level of security, but could also be easily recycled failed stringent security tests.

The new ticket stocks that state lotteries are switching to are highly biodegradable. Unlike the old ticket stock, which had bits of aluminum in it, environmentally friendly ticket stock will decompose in a relatively short time, similar to other types of paper.

In celebration of this new "friendly" paper, the Minnesota Lottery created a special new scratch-off game called Our Minnesota, which displayed five different Minnesota outdoor scenes created by Minnesota artist Keith Groves on the tickets. Take note of this, all you lottery tickets collectors out there: this is a highly desirable set of five tickets you will want to add to your collection.

PART VI

Those Incredible Winners and Losers!

"How difficult is it to falsify a winning lottery ticket and not get caught?"

Is there a lottery winner's curse?

Q: Does life really get easier and better for people who win giant lotto jackpots? It certainly doesn't seem like it from the things I read and hear. I just read in our paper this morning about another of our state's lottery winners who is deeply in debt and was forced to file bankruptcy. I keep reading about winners who seem to be in worse shape a couple of years after their big wins than they were before. I never hear about winners who are doing really well after their wins, but I hear all the time about winners who mess up somehow, go bankrupt, or even go to jail. What happens to these people? Is there some kind of lotto winner's curse that goes along with winning a lottery jackpot?

A: No, there is no curse, but there is the increased responsibility of dealing reasonably and rationally with a sudden increase in riches, and that is not easy for some winners. Unfortunately for many winners, winning the lottery does not bring any change of character or values. A poor money manager before winning the lottery will still be a poor money manager after the big win; a person with weak character or with questionable values before winning will have the same character flaws and dubious values after winning.

Did the person who bought $80,000 worth of lottery tickets for one drawing win anything?

Q: I'm curious about the guy we read about who reportedly bought $80,000 worth of lotto tickets in an attempt to win a giant Florida Lottery $88 million jackpot. Did he win? Did he win anything? I was actually tempted by all those millions to run out and borrow money and buy 10,000 tickets. Fortunately, or unfortunately perhaps, my wife wouldn't let me, and I only bought 10 tickets.

A: Count your blessings that you have a sensible wife.

In every state, whenever there is a giant jackpot there are always people who foolishly run out and buy thousands of dollars worth of lottery tickets in an attempt to capture all those millions of lottery dollars. So far, no one who has done this has won, and rarely has anyone come anywhere close to winning enough lower-tier prizes to pay back the money spent in the attempt to win the jackpot. Even spending thousands of dollars on lottery tickets, you just can't buy enough tickets to sway the odds in your favor. These incidents of temporary insanity by lottery players are foolish.

The Florida player you are referring to who spent $80,000 on lottery tickets (and who may have been representing a lottery pool) was not one of the six jackpot winners who split the $88 million jackpot. Even buying 80,000 tickets doesn't increase your chances in any significant way. Here's why.

In Florida's 6/49 game, there are 13,983,816 different number combinations, any of which could win the jackpot. This Florida player bought 80,000 of those possible combinations, but that still left over 13,900,000 other number combinations that could win. His 80,000 number combinations only amounted to about one-half of 1% of the total number combinations possible. That still left the probability of the winning ticket being in the other 99.5% of possible number combinations. Certainly, this player stood a better chance of winning with his 80,000 tickets than you did with your 10, but still the chances of him winning were very small.

Does lottery winning luck rub off?

Q: Did you hear anything about one lottery winner whose luck "rubbed off" on his friend who then also won the lottery? What is this stuff about luck rubbing off? Is there anything to it?

A: Of course there is. Every lottery player knows that if you can rub up against a previous lottery jackpot winner, some of his or her luck will rub off on you.

It happened to Andy Boehnlein in May 1993. He was working on a new house for Virginia Lotto winner Melvin Copeland, installing tile in the Copelands' kitchen. Andy frequently joked about "hoping some of the Copelands' luck will rub off on me." Little did he know how quickly that luck would rub off. Andy's quick-pick numbers came up when he was still working on the house. Andy won half of the $4.2 million Virginia Lottery jackpot on May 15, 1993. He didn't waste any time picking up his first check for $105,919. Now Andy says that people are trying to get his luck to rub off on them.

And then there is David Kuh. I spoke with David, who won the Michigan Lottery in 1985. He told me an interesting story. He had been laid off from work and was on unemployment. Times were pretty tough. But then his luck changed. He bought one lottery ticket and won $1.5 million, $55,000 a year after taxes for twenty years. David's best friend congratulated him, shook his hand and said, "Maybe some of your luck will rub off on me." A year later this friend won the Michigan Lottery. Meanwhile, seven guys who used to work with David before he got laid off contacted him and also wanted to shake his hand, thinking that some of David's luck might rub off on them. David obliged. The seven guys formed a lottery pool and played weekly. Guess what? You guessed it. Their pool won the Michigan Lottery also.

Don't forget Augustus Alvarez, who won over $2 million on April 6, 1991, in the Illinois Lottery. In April of 1990, he was working as a bellman at the Swissotel in Chicago where the annual Illinois Lottery Millionaires Reunion was being held. At that time he carried the bags of several lottery millionaires to their rooms. He said that one of the millionaires told him, "It will be your turn someday." Guess what. One year later Alvarez won, and just in time to attend the 1991 millionaires reunion back at his old place of employment, the Swissotel. But this time, his bags were carried to his room by other bellmen, former co-workers of his just a couple of weeks earlier.

Alvarez said, "Although I enjoyed assisting Illinois Lottery millionaires with their luggage at past reunions, I much prefer having my luggage carried for me." I can understand that.

So, does luck rub off? These winners say yes.

Who won the lottery while trying to prove you couldn't win the lottery?

Q: Do you know anything about someone in Indiana who was trying to point out that playing the lottery was a waste of money, and to prove it bought a lottery ticket—and won?

A: I believe you are referring to Craig Stanley of New Albany, Indiana. He was trying to give his children a lesson in frugality when it backfired on him. He had been trying to dissuade his family from buying lottery tickets, pointing out the majority of players never won anything and that "a fool and his money are soon parted." To prove his point, Stanley gave his family $1 to spend on a lotto ticket. His youngest son, Matt, promptly bought the winning ticket worth $1.25 million! "The only thing I can say right now is if you can't beat 'em, join 'em," declares Stanley. He now plans to start playing the lottery regularly.

But this story doesn't have a happy ending. Even though Stanley and his family won, they also ended up losers. After the Stanleys announced to the media—in detail—when they were planning their trip to lottery headquarters to claim the jackpot, trouble struck. The Stanleys arrived home after picking up their check to find that thieves had made good use of the time they were gone and had burglarized their home, making off with cash, jewelry and other valuables.

Lottery officials advise winners not to publicize any travel plans. I guess there are several lessons to be learned in this story.

What do big lottery winners buy with their millions?

Q: I know you've probably been asked this before, but what have lottery winners purchased with their millions? Have they bought anything or done anything really interesting?

A: Predictably, most winners pay off bills, buy a car, buy a new house, pay for college, help children and grandchildren, and take vacations—usually a cruise. That's what you'd expect from lottery winners. But have some winners done the unpredictable and spent their winnings on the outrageous, the extravagant, the decadent? I checked back over the five years of Florida's lottery winners and found that they had spent their money on the following slightly unusual expenditures: a time-share in Las Vegas, a new well, steps, a foundation "to assist young people with scholarships," a vacation home on a riverboat, sent a god-child's "husband to college, saved my house from foreclosure," a "beautiful princess wedding," an airplane, more lotto tickets, a color printer for a computer, expensive suits, a T.V., central heat and air, a solid gold Rolex, a catfish farm in North Carolina, a used car, a washer and dryer, dental work, a belated honeymoon, a 53-foot fishing yacht and a BMW, the company "where I used to work," a College Assistance Fund at church, a private school education, a jeep, and so on.

Surprised? The great majority of big lottery winners get real practical when they win. All of those extravagant dreams they had before they won get shelved. With the rare exception, lottery winners are a sensible bunch.

Did a couple really receive a multi-million-dollar lottery ticket for a wedding present?

Q: I just heard this lottery story and I want to know if it really happened. Do you know of a couple who got married and among the gifts was a lottery ticket, which turned out to be a winning ticket worth several million dollars?

A: It really happened.

While exchanging their vows, Britt and Pam Spangler were being turned into millionaires because a relative gave them an Illinois Lottery ticket as a wedding present that turned out to be worth $3 million.

I always tell my friends and family to give me lottery tickets as presents when they ask me what I want for Christmas or my birthday. Why not? I already have enough neckties.

What's the story on the Ohio Lottery winner who also won the Florida Lottery?

Q: What do you know about the guy who won the Ohio Lottery and then came to Florida and won the Florida Lottery? What's his story?

A: Some lottery players are just plain lucky. There is no other explanation for the winning experiences of 66-year-old Joseph Patrick Crowley who retired to Boca Raton in 1987 after he matched all six winning numbers in the Ohio Lottery and won $3 million. On December 25, 1993, Crowley won again, this time in the Florida Lottery, putting him in a very small group of about a dozen people who have won lottery top prizes twice. What was his winning amount this second time? An impressive $20 million.

It seems that Crowley had played some Florida instant games and won. When he cashed in a $50 winning ticket he bought 30 lotto tickets with the winnings, and one of those 30 had the winning combination. His Florida winnings from that winning ticket will pay him nearly $1 million a year for the next 20 years.

Crowley said that he fully intends to keep playing the Florida lottery, and that he is glad he ignored the advice of friends who told him not to waste money continuing to play the lottery because nobody ever won lotto twice.

I have a feeling that with Crowley's luck, he may just win again.

How can you win a pick-5 jackpot twice on the same day?

Q: Did you hear anything about some lottery player who accidentally won a pick-5 jackpot twice on the same day? I'm sure it can be done, but for the life of me I can't guess how it could, especially when I can't even get close to winning once.

A: Stanley Boraz of Missouri and his friend and employee Gene Cotton play the lottery sporadically, pooling their funds. They had been using quick pick and hadn't had much luck, so Stanley picked the five numbers and Gene went to the store to purchase the ticket for the day.

When Gene asked to purchase three days worth of tickets, the clerk accidently gave him one ticket for just one day. Gene said, "I noticed it and told him I really wanted one for three days." Instead of having the clerk cancel the first ticket, Gene purchased it also, along with another ticket for three days. He now had two tickets with the same numbers for the same day.

The next morning Gene read the winning numbers in the newspaper and was astounded to find that he had the winning numbers on the two duplicated tickets—two winning tickets! Each ticket was worth $100,000.

I keep saying that the best way to win a lottery prize is to buy a ticket that was a mistake in some way. These "mistakes" always seem to turn out to be winners.

And one last bit of information about Stanley and Gene. How do you think they split the $200,000? Fifty-fifty? No. The men have decided to split the $200,000 with Gene getting $120,000 and Stanley getting $80,000. Why? "We always planned on just splitting it even, but I felt like, as the employer, I should give some extra to Gene," Stanley said. Wow. That's my kind of boss.

Can illegal aliens win the lottery legally?

Q: Can illegal immigrants collect lottery winnings if they win a grand prize jackpot? I am from Guatemala and am in this country illegally. I have won a few small lottery prizes but am hoping I will one day win a jackpot.

A: Yes, occasionally illegal immigrants do win lottery jackpots and they are always allowed to keep their winnings. They are usually deported at the same time, however.

In November 1993, Conor and Elizabeth Murphy of Quincy, Massachusetts, won a Massachusetts Megabucks jackpot worth $3.5 million. The Murphys are from Ireland and are living in the U.S. illegally.

Currently, the Murphys are entered in a second lottery, a citizenship lottery being conducted by the federal government. They are very hopeful about this lottery also, because at least 40% of the visas to be awarded in the citizenship lottery by the State Department have been guaranteed to Irish applicants.

Is it true that a lottery director has gone to jail?

Q: I know that state lotteries have been surprisingly free from any hint of misconduct up until now, but that fairly recently one lottery director has been sentenced to prison. What for?

A: Two lottery officials from West Virginia have been sentenced to prison. Butch Bryan resigned as West Virginia Lottery Director in February 1993, when he was charged with insider trading, wire fraud, mail fraud and lying to a grand jury. Ed ReBrook was fired as lottery counsel in March 1993, when he was charged with insider trading and wire fraud. Bryan was sentenced to four years, and ReBrook was sentenced to two years.

Why was the law after a Colorado lottery winner?

Q: I understand that a Colorado Lottery winner has been sent to jail and still may be charged with additional crimes. What did this lottery winner do?

A: Albert Tecci won a $7 million Colorado Lottery jackpot and then promptly proceeded to spend his winnings on a cocaine habit and gambling. Not long before, Tecci had been released from a Massachusetts prison after serving part of an 18-month sentence for failure to pay child support, only to find himself back in hot water again. In April 1994, the state of Colorado sued both Tecci and his current wife, claiming the two established a complicated system of trusts and banking arrangements to make their lotto winnings "unreachable by his [Tecci's] ex-wife" and the states of Massachusetts and Colorado. Also in the same month, a Denver judge froze $54,293 in lottery payments to him until a trial can be held to determine whether the money should go to his children in Massachusetts or to an Arizona company that loaned Tecci $1.7 million in exchange for part of his winnings.

What does Tecci say about all this? He claims that he is now "turning my life back to where I am working hard, devoting my time to my current wife and son."

What happens to your lottery winnings when you go to jail?

Q: What can you tell me about the doctor in Pennsylvania who won the lottery and is now going to jail? What did he do? When someone wins the lottery and then goes to jail, what happens to the unreceived annual lottery payments?

A: This is another good example of how lottery jackpots are won by both the deserving and the undeserving.

You are referring to former chiropractor Bruce Brilliantine, 49, who pleaded guilty in May to charges of defrauding insurance companies out of nearly $70,000. Brilliantine was subsequently sentenced to 60 days in jail, four years probation, ordered to perform 200 hours of community service, and fined $515,000, including restitution to the insurance carriers. Brilliantine admitted to collecting the $70,000 in disability insurance from several carriers by falsifying records. Authorities said he submitted applications and 234 claims to companies for patients who never received treatment.

While the fraud charges were pending, he played and won the January 1992 New Jersey Pick-6 Lotto jackpot worth $12 million, although he didn't come forward until December 1992, nearly a year later, to collect the first installment of the prize—over $400,000. He showed up quietly at lottery headquarters, requesting that his name not be publicized.

Lottery officials say that future annual payments of over $400,000 will be paid to Brilliantine unless he defaults on his agreement to pay the fine. If that happened, the court would order his winnings confiscated until the fine was paid.

Has anyone actually gone to jail for ticket tampering?

Q: Has anybody ever gone to jail for trying to alter a lottery ticket in order to make it a winner? I know that many people try to do that and have been caught, but has anyone ever actually gone to jail?

A: Yes, lottery states prosecute with vigor people who attempt to cheat the lottery. State lotteries want to give the impression that it is a very dangerous thing to mess with. Not long ago, a woman in South Dakota was convicted of altering a ticket, trying to make it look like a big winner. She was sentenced to two years in prison and a $2,000 fine. That is about the average sentence for similar violations in other lottery states.

State lotteries now have the most sophisticated and foolproof security possible. Take, for example, the case of the two men in 1987 who made a good try and almost succeeded in falsely claiming a $15.2 million Pennsylvania jackpot.

For 10 months no one had claimed the $15 million prize, and the press was full of stories speculating on where the winning ticket might be. But, six weeks before the deadline for collecting the money, Mark Herbst, 33, stepped forward with the winning ticket. He said the ticket had been used as a bookmark and had been forgotten. All the publicity had made him go looking for it.

Herbst's ticket was validated, and Herbst was awarded the first of 25 installments, each worth $470,000. He went away a happy man.

Three days later, Herbst and his friend, Henry Rich, a computer repairman, were arrested and charged with theft, conspiracy, tampering with public records, forgery and unlawful use of a computer. It appears the mastermind Rich, a computer repairman who worked for the company that provides the lottery tickets and computer terminals for imprinting the tickets, stole a blank ticket, printed it with the correct numbers and date using a spare terminal at work, and then convinced his friend Herbst to turn it in.

Lottery officials won't tell how they discovered the ticket was false but they have tightened security considerably since then. Because of the fiasco, and because of security improvements, lottery officials state that the same scam probably couldn't be pulled off today in any lottery state.

Is it possible to "create" a winning ticket and not get caught?

Q: My friend was telling me the other day that he "doctored" a losing scratch-off ticket somehow, turned it in and was given $50 by a convenience store clerk. I said it was impossible to do. He said he'd show me sometime how he did it. What do you think? Is it possible to phony-up a winning ticket and not get caught?

A: First, your "friend" is a criminal and is putting you in a very bad position by telling you of his criminal activity. If he gets caught, and the odds are that he will be caught fairly quickly, he will go to jail. Authorities in lottery states take very seriously the tampering with and turning in of doctored tickets. There is extensive investigation of all lottery ticket counterfeiting or tampering.

Yes, it is possible to tamper with losing tickets and to illegally create "winning" scratch-off tickets. Some of the phony winning tickets are impossible to detect with the naked eye. But, if the clerk who redeems the ticket is doing his or her job, it will be impossible to collect on the ticket because there are so many safeguards built into the redemption process. Phony tickets do still get turned in and money does get paid occasionally, but only if the clerks fail to do everything required of them by the lottery. If clerks get pressured, busy or forgetful, they sometimes don't do what they are supposed to do, and a doctored ticket gets redeemed. In those cases, the lottery will not reimburse the store for the money it paid out on those "bad" tickets.

It might be a good idea to distance yourself from this "friend." It sounds like he is living dangerously.

How was the man planning to bribe lottery officials?

Q: Do you know anything about the man in Louisiana who was arrested for trying to bribe the Louisiana Lottery officials to let him win? How was he planning to accomplish this little endeavor?

A: I don't think he really had much of a plan, just a desire to win. William Swearingen, 53, a truck driver from Crawley, Louisiana, says that all he wanted to do was split millions of dollars with Louisiana Lottery officials. What's so bad about that? And all officials had to do to get these millions was to rig the drawings to let Swearingen win the multi-million-dollar jackpot twice. Swearingen would keep the first jackpot and then divide up the second jackpot among cooperating lottery officials. For some strange reason, lottery officials didn't like this foolproof winning idea and now Swearingen faces up to five years in prison and a $1,000 fine for attempted bribery.

Are there any winners who only buy one ticket?

Q: I like to read about people who win the lottery, but since I only spend $1 a week playing Lotto, I especially like to read about people who win when they only purchase one ticket. I guess it gives me hope. Have there been any one-ticket winners lately?

A: There are dozens of one-ticket players who win everyday. We don't read about them very often because there is too much other more dramatic lottery information. But just to keep you encouraged, here are two $1 winners that I enjoyed hearing about.

Seventy-year-old Coos Bay, Oregon, resident William Dee, who plays one set of numbers each week, won the March 6 Oregon Powerball prize for matching all five regular numbers. He won the $100,000 prize. So what's so special about that, you are probably wondering, lots of people win $100,000 every week with one ticket purchases. That's correct, but it's what Mr. Dee purchased with his winnings that was fun. He bought a new pick-up truck so that he could drive to Alaska and Arkansas to visit his buddies. He was planning to use his old truck for the trip but decided not to now that he could afford to buy a new one. He figured he had babied his old truck long enough and it could retire. It had over 342,000 miles on it.

And then there is the Cameron, Missouri, woman, Millie Bond, 61, who decided to play the Missouri Powerball game for the first time. She bought one ticket just hours before the drawing. And did she ever win! She correctly picked all six winning numbers and will receive $1.5 million—every year for 20 years! It seems that Millie won the largest jackpot prize in Missouri Lottery history.

You've heard it before: $1 is all it takes to win a large lottery jackpot.

How many lottery millionaires have been created?

Q: How many people have become millionaires because they won the lottery?

A: It is hard to know exactly, because frequently the annual income from one winning ticket for a giant jackpot may be split between several family members thereby making each of them a millionaire, even though lottery records only count the actual owner of the ticket as the winner and the millionaire. We do know that there are at least 10,000 "lotto millionaires" that have been created since lotteries began in the '60s. We have so many lotteries in operation (37 at the moment) that we now are creating new millionaires at the rate of more than 1000 a year. That's more than three new lottery millionaires every day!

Do pools ever win smaller prizes in amounts large enough to share?

Q: I know that you recommend forming lottery pools as the best way to increase your chances of winning the lottery grand prize, but the likelihood of winning it is still small even when you are part of a pool. But what about winning 5-of-6, 4-of-6, or 3-of-6 prizes? Do pools ever win smaller prizes in amounts large enough to share among all the pool members?

A: Pools frequently win lower-tier prizes even if they don't win the lottery grand prize, and often the total of those smaller wins is significant.

For example, on March 9, 1991, a pool of 17 co-workers in Virginia won 65 prizes in one lotto drawing. The pool usually buys between 170 and 250 tickets for each drawing and frequently wins lower-tier prizes. For the March 9 drawing the group really got lucky. They had four 5-of-6 combinations ($1,215 each), 30 4-of-6 ($53 each), and 31 3-of-6 (free play for each).

How were the number combinations selected? Pool members picked their own numbers.

Why did the lottery winner get arrested—and not have bail money?

Q: Do you know anything about a $5 million lottery winner who got arrested and didn't have the money for bail? Where did the money go? What did he or she get arrested for?

A: Not all lottery winners live happily ever after. Most do, but not all.

Minus Cole Jr. won $5.4 million (that is $250,000 a year before taxes) in the Illinois Lottery in September 1988. On April 15, 1991, Cole was arrested and charged with attempted murder and aggravated battery in which he allegedly shot and wounded his girlfriend and her son. Bail was set at $500,000, but several days afterward he was still being held in jail because he couldn't make bail.

Where did the money go? Who knows?

Have twins ever each won the lottery?

Q: My twin sister and I are both avid lottery players. We have this feeling both of us are going to win the lottery some day. Are you aware of any sisters who have each won the lottery independently of each other, or will we be the first?

A: You won't be the first.

Three years after her sister won a $1.8 million Massachusetts Lottery jackpot, Phyllis Ravenell won an almost identical amount playing the same game. Phyllis and her sister, Barbara Dupuis, each won almost exactly the same prize, just three years apart. That's about as strange a double win among sisters as I've heard of.

Should a mob boss be allowed to win the lottery?

Q: What do you think about the guy in Massachusetts, who is supposedly some kind of organized crime boss, who won over $14 million in the Massachusetts Lottery? Do you think he should be allowed to collect it? I don't! After all, he is supposed to be involved with drug trafficking, gambling and other racketeering activities.

A: I think that if he has a winning ticket, he should collect his winnings just like anyone else. It's a good thing that winners of lottery prizes don't have to be of high moral character. Too many of us would be unable to collect our winnings if we won.

State lotteries are doing the right thing by maintaining that anyone who signs the winning ticket gets paid the winnings. Period. Let the media speculate, and the law enforcement officials and the courts determine who's a criminal and who isn't, but keep the lottery out of it.

Do lottery winners really keep their jobs?

Q: Do lottery jackpot winners really keep their jobs and keep working? It seems that nearly everyone in the past few months who has won has declared that they are going to keep their jobs.

I'm more than a little skeptical. Do they actually keep working? I'd retire immediately if I won.

A: In spite of what they say in the first few exciting days of finding out they have won the lottery, people who win less than $2 million usually keep their jobs. People who win over $2 million usually quit work within a few weeks of collecting their first winning check.

Keep in mind that winning a million dollars really doesn't make you a millionaire, able to do whatever you want to do. A million dollar win amounts to about $35,000 a year for 20 years after taxes have been taken out. That's not really enough money each year to significantly change a person's lifestyle. Even winning $2 million only gives you about $70,000 a year.

Winners of over $2 million frequently believe that they will keep working, but they usually don't. A person who wins $5 million, for example, will quickly discover that a new income of $175,000 a year takes a considerable amount of time to manage it well. Suddenly the $25,000 a year job, even though a great job, doesn't seem quite that important anymore.

Mrs. Lorraine Greenwood, a New Hampshire Lottery winner who won $7 million on October 16, 1991, may have set a national record for the shortest time on the job after becoming a lottery winner. She was supposed to start a new job with the U.S. Postal Service on October 23, a job she had wanted for years, but after figuring how much money she was going to receive each year for the next 20 years—$250,000 after taxes— she called her new employer to announce her retirement, four days before she even started!

What happened to the South Dakota Lottery "winner" who died a day after he found out that he couldn't collect the winnings?

Q: Do you know anything about a man in South Dakota who won several million dollars in the lottery, and then died a day after he found out that there had been some mistake and he couldn't collect his winnings?

A: Woodrow and Lois Nelson, an elderly couple from Watertown, South Dakota, thought they owned the winning Lotto America Ticket worth $12 million, but it turned out to be a mistake. The Nelsons held the ticket that matched all six numbers shown on the lottery computer, but due to a lottery employee proofreading error, one of those numbers entered in the lottery's computer was wrong. The Nelsons were contacted later by the lottery and told of the mistake. They were told that they only won $1,095 instead of the $12 million.

Less than 24 hours after the discovery, Woodrow Nelson, 73, died of a heart attack. His wife Lois declined to comment on whether the computer error was linked to her husband's death. She did say that she believed she and her husband should have been awarded the jackpot amount.

Do truly needy people ever win the lottery?

Q: Do truly needy people ever win lottery jackpots?

A: I believe that anyone lucky enough to pick winning lotto numbers deserves to win, but that does not always make them "needy" people. Fortunately, however, many of the winners are also deserving and needy people.

Mark Beeks is a good example of this. Beeks had been unemployed since being discharged by the Navy in December 1992, when he won a $16.8 million California Super Lotto prize in a November 24, 1993, drawing. He had been drawing unemployment checks since the Navy discharged the former machinist's mate who had served 16 years. Beeks had no immediate plans for his yearly checks of $843,000 for 20 years, other than to "kick back."

Why worry about being too old to collect all your winnings?

Q: I'm 86 years old and am an avid lottery player here in Missouri. In fact, I've already made my plans for how to spend my fortune for the next 20 years when I get it. And I don't even care if it is paid to me over a 20-year period because I don't plan to die until I have collected it all and spent every cent of it. And maybe when that time comes, I'll decide to win another jackpot and hang around for another 20 years until I've spent that fortune also. Tell your older readers to stop worrying about the lottery paying them over a 20-year period and start making plans to spend their money. It'll keep them young.

A: And when you win, you'll have the distinction of being the oldest lottery winner in Missouri. The current oldest Missouri winner is Omer Williamson, a mere 85 years young. He won in January of 1992. Good luck.

PART VII

You're Playing the Wrong Game!

Did you know that it is actually one hundred times easier to win West Virginia Lotto than to win California Lotto?

Which state lotto games have the best odds?

Q: Which state's lotto has the best chances of winning, or are they all about the same difficulty?

A: There is quite a difference in lotto game odds from state to state—and even within the same state. Two states, Wisconsin and Massachusetts, offer two different lotto games with different chances of winning on different nights of the week. Some states offer a lotto game that is fairly easy to win, while others make it very tough to win. For example, it is a hundred times easier to win West Virginia Lotto than to win California Lotto.

The following list of state lotto games—listed in ascending order of difficulty—shows you the numbers you have to choose from and the corresponding odds of winning. Keep in mind, however, that as a general rule the easier a lotto game is to win, the smaller the jackpot. Winning a low-odds lotto jackpot may get you a top prize of $25,000, while winning a high-odds jackpot may get you a $25 million jackpot.

STATE	FIELD	ONE TICKET EQUALS
West Virginia	6 out of 25	1 chance in 177,100
Vermont	6 out of 30	1 chance in 593,775
Kansas	6 out of 33	1 chance in 1,107,568
Delaware	6 out of 36	1 chance in 1,947,792
New Hampshire	6 out of 36	1 chance in 1,947,792
Oneida Nation	6 out of 36	1 chance in 1,947,792
Wisconsin	6 out of 36	1 chance in 1,947,792
District of Columbia	6 out of 39	1 chance in 3,262,623
Iowa	6 out of 39	1 chance in 3,262,623
Tri-State (Vermont, Maine, New Hampshire)	6 out of 40	1 chance in 3,838,380
Tri-West (Idaho, Montana, North Dakota)	6 out of 41	1 chance in 4,496,388
Arizona	6 out of 42	1 chance in 5,245,786
Colorado	6 out of 42	1 chance in 5,245,786

Massachusetts	6 out of 42	1 chance in 5,245,786
Connecticut	6 out of 44	1 chance in 7,059,052
Indiana	6 out of 44	1 chance in 7,059,052
Louisiana	6 out of 44	1 chance in 7,059,052
Oregon	6 out of 44	1 chance in 7,059,052
Virginia	6 out of 44	1 chance in 7,059,052
Georgia	6 out of 46	1 chance in 9,366,819
New Jersey	6 out of 46	1 chance in 9,366,819
Ohio	6 out of 47	1 chance in 10,737,573
Pennsylvania	6 out of 48	1 chance in 12,271,512
Missouri	6 out of 48	1 chance in 12,271,512
Florida	6 out of 49	1 chance in 13,983,816
Kentucky	6 out of 49	1 chance in 13,983,816
Massachusetts	6 out of 49	1 chance in 13,983,816
Maryland	6 out of 49	1 chance in 13,983,816
Wisconsin	6 out of 49	1 chance in 13,983,816
Michigan	6 out of 49	1 chance in 13,983,816
Washington	6 out of 49	1 chance in 13,983,816
Texas	6 out of 50	1 chance in 15,890,700
California	6 out of 51	1 chance in 18,009,460
Illinois	6 out of 54	1 chance in 25,827,165
New York	6 out of 54	1 chance in 25,827,165
Powerball	5 out of 45 +	
	1 out of 45	1 chance in 55,000,000

What numbers are played most frequently in daily cash games?

Q: What numbers are played the most in the daily cash games? If I can find out what they are, I'll stay away from those numbers so I don't have to share with so many others if I win.

A: I think that you are a bit confused about how the daily cash game prizes are paid. In most states it is only lotto and the pick-5 game that pays winners on a parimutuel basis. This means that the jackpot pool amount is divided equally among the winners. If you play one of the popular lotto combinations when it is drawn, you will split with a large number of other players. But, for the daily pick-3 and pick-4 games, when the winning numbers are drawn, a set amount is paid to each winner no matter how many winners there are, so it doesn't matter if many winners have the same numbers, you will not have to share the prize amount. As a matter of fact, in every state lottery, when popular number combinations are drawn in a pick-3 or a pick-4 game, frequently the payouts are three, four, or five times the amount that players wagered on that game. In Virginia, in October 1992, the numbers 222 were drawn in the pick-3 game. Players won $3.7 million on just $706,000 in wagers that day, the highest pick-3 payout recorded for the state. The previous highest payout was $3.4 million when 333 was drawn. Incidentally, players love it when they break the lottery bank for any game.

So what numbers are played the most in these games? According to records kept for every state lottery, the popular numbers are the same in each state. For pick-3 games, the most popular numbers are triple numbers such as 111, 222, 333, and so on. Next are the day's date and the numbers 123. For the pick-4 games, the most popular numbers are usually quadruples (such as 4444) and 1010, 1020, 1212, and 1234.

Can you play all zeros in pick-3 and pick-4 games?

Q: When you play the pick-3 or pick-4 games, can you pick multiple zeros for your numbers, such as 0-0-0 or 0-0-0-0, or must you play numbers with value, such as 1-2-3-4?

A: Yes, you may choose all zeros if you wish. Not long ago, Sam Abdo, a Florida Lottery player, used his lucky numbers, 0-0-0-0, to win a play-4 game when those were the numbers drawn for that game. All zero numbers are just as likely to be drawn as numbers such as 2-2-2-2, 4-5-6-7, 8-9-9-8 or any other set of numbers.

Will you explain the many ways to win playing pick-3?

Q: I'm a little confused by the ways that a lottery player can win when playing our state's daily pick-3 game. It appears that there are several ways to win—even when you pick just two numbers! Or is this a different game altogether—a daily pick-2 game? I haven't played the pick-3 because I don't understand it, but I'm told that the odds are much better than with lotto.

A: Your chances of winning are significantly better in your daily pick-3 game than in lotto, but remember that the prizes are also much smaller than those won in lotto.

I don't have enough space in this book to explain all the pick-3 variations, but I will describe a few. You can read more about pick-3 wagering by picking up a pick-3 "How To Play" brochure where you buy your lottery tickets. But in summary, here's how it works.

In most states with daily pick-3 games, the minimum ticket price is 50¢, but the player may bet more on a single pick. For example, if you bet $1 on a three-number pick and those numbers win, you will win twice as much as you would have won if you had only bet 50¢.

The simplest way to play is called a straight bet. You simply choose three digits between 0 and 9. You win if the numbers selected are drawn in the same order as your numbers. Your chances of winning with a straight bet are 1 in 1000. The largest prizes are given for this win.

Another way to wager is to use a six-way box, sometimes called an any-order bet. With this bet you pick three different numbers (such as 5, 6, 7) and you win if those numbers are drawn in any order (675, 765, etc.). Since there are six different combinations of those three numbers, your chances of winning are six times better than with a straight bet. Since the odds of winning with this bet are 1 in 167, the payout is only about one-sixth as large as a straight bet. Got the idea?

Now what about those two-number bets? Some states offer a pick-3 option called pair variations. Instead of picking three numbers, you choose two numbers and leave the third space blank. You may pick the first two numbers (front pair), the last two numbers (back pair), or in some states, the first and last numbers (split pair). You win if your two numbers are drawn in the positions you selected. Your chances of winning something with the "pair" bets are very good, 1 in 100. These are, in effect, pick-2 numbers games, but made part of the pick-3 games for the sake of convenience and to avoid player confusion.

How long before I win at pick-3 when I play the same numbers every day?

Q: I have been playing the same three numbers (509) in our state's pick-3 game five times a week for the last four years, and I haven't yet won. Isn't that a little weird? Shouldn't I have won at least once in all those attempts? What about the law of averages?

A: Yes, that's a little weird, but not unheard of. Playing the same three numbers over a long period of time like you did generally results in those numbers being selected a time or two at least—but not always.

For example, the Virginia Lottery just finished its fifth year of pick-3 games. During those five years, three sets of numbers were actually drawn six times: 133, 246, 703. Fourteen sets of numbers were drawn five times: 222, 269, 272, 283, 426, 427, 464, 509, 522, 548, 646, 763, 891, 924. Note that your numbers, 509, were drawn 5 times in this pick-3 game. Your problem is that you are playing in the wrong state.

By the way, there was one set of numbers that was never

drawn during the past five years: 000. But then again, someone might argue that 000 isn't really a number anyway.

Will my winning pick-3 numbers win again?

Q: I just won a pick-3 drawing. I had been playing the same numbers every day for about three months, and they finally came in. My question is this: Should I continue to play these same three numbers or is it unlikely that they will win again for a long time?

A: Your chances of having your same three numbers in exact order on any one day are 1 in 1000. The chances are pretty good that your numbers will come up again, maybe even the next day.

Surprisingly to most lottery players who are used to the same set of winning lotto numbers never being drawn again, it is not uncommon for the same three numbers to be drawn two days in a row. In most lottery states this happens every year or two. The Maryland Lottery just had it happen on August 6 and August 7, 1993, when the number 645 was drawn both days. Although the odds of that number appearing two days in a row are one in a million, it does happen. In Maryland, it happened three times in 1991.

Have the same pick-3 numbers ever been drawn two days in a row?

Q: Have the same pick-3 numbers ever been drawn two days in a row? What are the chances of this happening?

A: The odds of any state lottery drawing the same three numbers in a pick-3 game two days in a row are one in a million, but it has happened from time to time.

For example, the Maryland Lottery had the same numbers drawn back-to-back three times since the Maryland Pick-3 game began in 1976: 594 on February 12 and 13, 1982; 011 on March 3 and 4, 1982; and 639 on January 26 and 27, 1991.

Although it doesn't happen very often that the same numbers appear two days in a row, it can happen. Remember, any set of numbers has just the same chance of being drawn as any other set of numbers. That is what makes the lottery a game of chance rather than a game of skill.

What is a keno-type lottery game?

Q: I just came back from a trip to Kansas where the big lottery game seems to be keno, a game that players play all day long with drawings every five minutes or so. It seems to have captured the enthusiasm of lottery players because nearly every person I talked to eventually steered the conversation around to the subject of this keno lottery game and how much they had won or lost. What's so different about this lottery game and how is it played?

A: First played in China more than 3,000 years ago, keno is the world's oldest lottery game and has been played in casinos in the United States for decades. Keno lottery games are currently offered in several states (Oregon, California, Kansas, Rhode Island, Maryland), with several more states considering adding them in the near future. Where keno has been offered in other states, there has been substantial player interest. Why?

Keno-type games—basically electronic instant games—are so popular because they offer a large selection of ways to play, high probability of winning, lots of winners, big prizes, and the ability to quickly determine winners. A good example of a successful keno game is "Club Keno," the one you heard about operated by the Kansas Lottery.

Club Keno players can win up to $100,000 in cash prizes every five minutes. Tickets can be purchased seven days a week from 6 a.m. until 11:50 p.m. wherever lottery tickets are sold. To play the game, players choose from 10 different Club Keno options—one spot, four spot, ten spot, etc. For example, if you decide to play a four spot, you only select four numbers between 1 and 80. The lottery computer randomly selects 20 numbers. You win if two, three or four of your numbers are selected. Players can wager between $1 and $5 for each draw. The more wagered, the higher the prize. You either pick your own numbers or use the quick pick option and let the terminal select your numbers for you. Players decide how many consecutive drawings to enter—from 1 to 100. Probably the main attraction of this game is that Club Keno offers 214 drawings daily.

Players give their play slips to the retailer to be entered into the lottery on-line terminal, the wager is collected and players are given a computer-issued ticket. Once you receive your ticket, you can check your numbers to see if you are a winner on the television monitors in the store. The winning numbers are selected by a special lottery computer programmed to randomly select numbers every five minutes, not by a lottery hostess drawing ping-pong balls out of a drawing machine. But what if you can't watch the drawings in the store all day long? How do you know if you've won anything? Simple. You can check your numbers later on the in-store display system or the retailer can also check your ticket through the terminal, which will tell you if any of your numbers were winners.

In states where keno has been tried—such as Oregon, Rhode Island, Michigan, and Kansas—players have been very enthusiastic about the game. Several lottery states are currently evaluating the concept for their players.

Which lottery states offer a keno game?

Q: Which lottery states now offer keno?

A: The following lottery states now offer keno. Note the differing number of keno numbers that the player may select, the number of keno numbers the lottery draws, and the different sizes of the number fields from which players have to choose their numbers.

STATE	PLAYER CHOOSES	LOTTERY DRAWS	SIZE OF FIELD
California	10 numbers	20 numbers	80 numbers
Colorado	10 numbers	20 numbers	60 numbers
Kansas	10 numbers	20 numbers	80 numbers
Maryland	10 numbers	20 numbers	80 numbers
Massachusetts	12 numbers	20 numbers	80 numbers
Michigan	10 numbers	22 numbers	80 numbers
New York	10 numbers	20 numbers	80 numbers
Oregon	10 numbers	20 numbers	80 numbers
Pennsylvania	7 numbers	10 numbers	74 numbers
Rhode Island	10 numbers	20 numbers	80 numbers
Washington	10 numbers	20 numbers	80 numbers

What is Powerball all about?

Q: I keep reading and hearing a lot about some fantastic "Powerball" lottery that is being played in several states and it has even had a $100 million jackpot as well as several other big ones. We don't have Powerball in our state, but I'd sure like to know about it. What can you tell me?

A: Powerball is a multi-state lotto-type game that is offered by 15 states with relatively small populations that have combined to offer this lotto game. The combination of the 15 state population player base and the relative difficulty of winning the Powerball jackpot combine to create occasional giant jackpots.

When that occurs, the media make it appear that giant Powerball jackpots are a regular occurrence when they are not.

In the states that offer Powerball, players may play two games a week. Drawings are held on Wednesday and Saturday, with a minimum jackpot each drawing of $2 million. Powerball jackpots roll over frequently but seldom get larger than $20 million. And the odds of winning the jackpot are awful, the worst in the country. In fact, they are so bad that I wonder why people even try to win. The odds of winning the Powerball jackpot are 55 million to one. The lotto odds are long in many states, but they are a whole lot better than Powerball. A 6/49 lotto has odds of 1 in 14 million of winning the jackpot.

In order to win the jackpot in Powerball, you must choose six numbers correctly, but there is a difference. During the twice weekly televised drawings, two drawing drums are used. You must choose five numbers from one set of 45 numbers and then you choose the sixth number (the powerball) from another set of 45 numbers. Instead of having these six numbers selected out of one drawing machine, two sets of numbers are used and drawings are made from two different machines. You have to correctly guess six numbers from a total of 90 numbers. That's what makes the odds so long.

Players do like Powerball, though, even if they don't win the jackpot, because there are eight other ways to win prizes. If you win with 5 of 5 but not the powerball, you win $100,000. Your odds here are 1,249,526 to 1. Not bad odds. You can win $5,000, $100, $5, $2 or $1 with fewer numbers. You even win if you have one correct number.

Can you tell me about a new high-tech lottery game where you pick dates, not numbers?

Q: Have you heard of a new high-tech lottery game where instead of picking a set of numbers you pick a date—I think a month, day, and year—and then play that date? How is this

played? Which state lottery offers this game? How much can you win?

A: You are referring to the Minnesota Lottery's game, DATO!, the first really new type of lottery game that has been dreamed up by any state lottery in a long time. DATO! is designed to appeal to those millions of players who already regularly play special "lucky number" dates when they play lotto.

With DATO!, players simply fill in a play slip with a month, day and the last two digits of a year—past, present or future. They win the top prize of $5,000 if their month, day and year are the same numbers randomly selected by a lottery computer. Players can also win smaller prizes. They win $1 if they just pick the correct month, $3 if they only pick the correct day, $5 if they pick the correct year, $25 if they guess the correct month and day, $50 for the correct month and year, and $150 if they guess the day and year. Chances of winning the top prize of $5000 are 1 in 36,525; overall chances of winning something range from 1:8.1 to 1:9.1 depending on the date played.

Even the twice a week drawings for DATO! are different and fun because winning dates are not on ping-pong balls bouncing around in the familiar drawing machine we are used to seeing on television. Instead, the lottery uses a specially developed computer program to select the winning date. Behind the scenes, this computer-selected winning date is then simultaneously entered into a special computer. Through a complex set of computations, the program instantaneously tells an animation program what date to enter. What viewers see on television is a first-of-its-kind computer-animated drawing that gives viewers a sense of traveling through the polished bronze and copper gears and sprockets of a time machine. This 12-second animated trip through the machine ends with the winning date being stamped on a chunk of metal in the midst of moving gear wheels. This animated number-picking uses the same high-tech animation used to produce the Coca-Cola polar bear commercials and the animation for Steven Spielberg's *Jurassic Park*.

Can scratch-off tickets be used for buying groceries?

Q: Is it true that some state lotteries are offering instant ticket games where after you scratch off the ticket you can use it to get discounts on groceries in the same manner that shoppers now use coupons to get cents off on different products? If this is true, I think it is a great idea. It would be that much more of an incentive for me to play the lottery, especially the scratch-off games.

A: In 1993, the Pennsylvania Lottery offered an instant game called "Cookout Cash," which offered cash prizes as well as cents-off coupon discounts for specified grocery products.

On each instant game ticket, along with the possibility of winning cash, players received coupon discounts ranging from 20¢ to 50¢ off a grocery purchase. But the offer was limited. All the discount coupons were for cookout related products such as Campbell's Pork & Beans, Vlasic Pickles, Snyder's of Hanover pretzels, Dietz & Watson Beef or Meat Franks, Wampler-Longacre Turkey Burgers and Wampler-Longacre Chicken or Turkey Franks, and all the brands were Pennsylvania food producers. Lottery officials say that the food coupons represented $6 million in additional prize value to players.

Response of players was enthusiastic. Other state lotteries will probably create similar games. Each lottery is always looking for innovative new games that will excite player interest and give players the biggest possible return on each $1 wagered. With games like this Pennsylvania game, players benefit, the lottery still gives the same amount of money in prizes, and the manufacturers get their money's worth in free advertising and increased sales.

How can a winning scratch-off ticket be worth $17 million?

Q: Do you know anything about the person who bought a scratch-off ticket and won $17 million? I didn't know that you could win that much in the instant games.

A: You can't—at least, not yet.

I believe that you are referring to 83-year-old Walter Zachanki who bought an Illinois instant game ticket and won $2. He took $1 of his winnings and, using the quick pick system, bought a ticket for the lotto drawing of October 3, 1990. That ticket won the jackpot worth $17 million.

A $20 lottery ticket?

Q: Do you know anything about a Canadian lottery game in which each ticket costs $20? A friend of mine who recently visited Canada said that there was such a game. That seems like an unusually high-priced game.

A: Your friend was talking about one of the games conducted by Canada's Interprovincial Lottery Corporation. These high-priced "Special Edition" games are offered periodically with limited numbers of tickets available for short periods of time and with substantially bigger jackpots than other Canadian games.

One "Special Edition" game that I am familiar with offered only three million tickets for sale at $20 dollars each, but over $25 million was awarded in prizes. The interesting thing about this game was that each ticket was a "hybrid" ticket, entering the ticket holder in instant games as well as six lotto-like drawings. Players could win cash prizes from $1,000 to $5 million, plus luxury items such as South American cruises and Mercedes Benz and Lincoln Continental automobiles.

How much money was won in "El Gordo"?

Q: How much money was won in this year's giant "El Gordo" lottery in Spain? When I lived in Spain I used to play every year. Our family looked forward to the annual drawing more than to Christmas.

A: And I can understand that. This past year, the 102nd annual El Gordo ("the Fat One"), the world's richest one-time-a-year lottery, gave away over $1 billion on December 22, 1993, to thousands of very happy winners. The top prize 108 series (each series is comprised of 66,000 tickets) were each worth $2,140,000 for a total of $231,120,000. The 108 second prize series of tickets were each worth $1,029,000 for a total of $111,132,000. The 108 third prize series of tickets were each worth $514,300 for a total of $55,543,000. In addition to these big prizes, often shared by whole villages, there were many smaller prizes.

Why offer a $5 scratch-off game?

Q: What's this I hear about a $5 scratch-off ticket? Why is it so expensive? Why would any lottery want to sell such an expensive instant game, and why would anyone want to buy it? If I am going to spend $5, it makes more sense to play lotto.

A: Many people have a remarkably narrow view of scratch-off games, believing that all scratch-off games have a responsibility to cost no more than $1. Did you know that several states sell instant games that cost $2 or $3 a ticket?

The $5 instant game you are referring to was the Minnesota Lottery's "Instant Millions" scratch-off game and was the first ever $5 instant game offered by a U.S. lottery. This alone makes it a collector's dream and a desirable ticket to own, whether you win or not. Contrary to what you thought about a game that costs this much, this limited edition instant game became an overnight success with Minnesota Lottery players, and for some very good reasons besides its uniqueness.

The oversized ticket (three times the size of the usual instant game ticket) had some very appealing qualities. It had three separate scratch-off games on it, each with its own separate jackpots and game odds. Game 1 offered players a chance to win a million dollars instantly, a rare experience nowadays with instant games. Game 2 offered players the chance to win $25, and Game 3 offered players the chance of winning $1000.

Another of the very appealing features of this game were the relatively low odds. In fact, they were the lowest overall odds of any scratch-off game in the world! Chances of winning a cash prize of some amount were very good—one in 2.96.

Incidentally, there were only eight million game tickets printed, about one-third the number usually printed for an instant game, and those sold fast.

Why aren't instant games more complicated?

Q: Why aren't instant game tickets a little more complicated? They are over too fast when you scratch them. Is there a scratch-off ticket that has multiple games on it? I've only seen instant games with one area to scratch off, but a friend tells me that he has played instant games where there were four separate latex areas to scrape off. I'd like to see a game like this. Do they exist?

A: Yes. Many states have instant games with two or three scratch-off areas—but you are correct, they aren't very complicated. A Minnesota Lottery ticket, "Beat The Dealer," was about as complicated as I have seen yet. It was similar to blackjack. Players started by scratching off their four separate card hands and then scratched off the dealer's hand. If the sum of the player's cards in any of the four games was higher than the sum of the dealer's game, the player won the corresponding prize for that game. The prize amount was printed below each game hand.

Lotteries don't like to make their instant games complicated because they want players to play them quickly without needing too much explanation. For most players, simple is better than complicated.

Does any state lottery conduct frequent second chance drawings?

Q: Does any state lottery conduct second chance drawings on a regular basis? Our state lottery used to have weekly second chance drawings when the lottery first started, but now we only have one every three months or so. I like the second chance drawings because the chances of having your ticket get selected are really pretty good compared to the chances of winning in lotto.

A: Lotteries use second chance drawings frequently when they start up because the second chance contests encourage people to buy more tickets. After all, even a non-winning ticket might win you something. But as games get established and as player patterns are formed, lotteries don't need to keep offering these second chance drawings to motivate people and the frequency of these contests lessens.

South Dakota gets my vote for the best second chance drawing at the moment. Because the population of South Dakota is small compared with the big lottery states, the chances of winning something in the drawing are very good because there are so many fewer tickets in each drawing, somewhere around 50,000.

To enter, players need to send in any five non-winning South Dakota Lottery instant scratch tickets in a standard letter envelope. One of the tickets in the envelope must have the player's name, address and telephone number printed on the back. As is the case with most second chance drawings, the envelope is not even opened until it is drawn and then it is opened to make certain that there are five tickets inside and to see what the owner's name and address is. Frequently when an envelope is opened, officials find out that the sender forgot to sign one of the tickets, and there is no way to determine who the sender is. The envelope and tickets are thrown away and another envelope is drawn.

What do winners win and how frequently are the drawings held? The lottery gives away 10 prizes of $1000 when each drawing is held on the last Thursday of each month. Where does the prize money come from? The drawing is financed by prize money that goes unclaimed throughout the year.

Which lottery gives away movies and cassette tapes when you lose?

Q: Which state lottery is offering a lottery game where you win movies or cassette tapes if you don't win money? It sounds like my kind of game.

A: Several different lotteries have found that giving away movies and cassettes is a successful promotion for instant games, and they give them away periodically. The Virginia Lottery offered a game not too long ago called MOVIES, MUSIC & MONEY, and players loved it even though not everyone won.

It's really two games in one. First, players scratched the top of the play areas. If they matched three dollar amounts, they could win a free ticket or up to $500. If they don't match, they had a second play area to scratch and a second chance to win a bonus ticket good toward their choice of more than 200 popular videos, CDs and cassettes described in special catalogs available at lottery retailer outlets. If "Bonus Win, Collect Tickets" appeared on the ticket, players collected anywhere from two to ten "merchandise" tickets and used those tickets as money to "buy" their choice of tapes or CDs in the catalog. Chances of winning something were really great. Overall chances of winning a prize, either money, movies, or music, were 1 in 2.7. These are about the best odds in the country.

How can I buy tickets for the Irish Sweepstakes lottery?

Q: How can I buy tickets for the famous Irish Sweepstakes? I haven't heard anything about it for years and don't have any idea how I can go about buying a ticket or two.

A: I'm sorry to disappoint you, but there is no Irish Sweepstakes anymore. The Irish Sweepstakes is gone forever, but now you can participate in its replacement, the Irish National Lottery which conducts a 6/39 lotto. Several companies sell these tickets. One of them is Regal Service Bureau, 1-800-367-9681.

The Irish National Lottery is unique because 15% of revenues are added from each draw to a special prize fund that is used to "pump up" the jackpot at the lottery's discretion. As a result, the jackpot often jumps by large amounts from week to week. All prizes are lump-sum and tax-free in Ireland. Good luck.

Do you know anything about a lottery-sponsored treasure hunt?

Q: Do you know anything about a search for hidden treasure conducted by a state lottery where players actually found some sort of treasure somewhere in the state? Apparently local radio

stations gave out clues each week. If sounds like fun, and I'd like to know more about it.

A: During the summer of 1993, the Oregon Lottery conducted an "Oregon Hidden Treasures" promotion that offered $1,000 in cash to each of the 20 people who could find a hidden medallion and bring it to lottery headquarters.

Oregon Lottery enthusiasts put their best detective skills to work in trying to find the treasure medallions hidden in 20 different places around the state. One radio station in each area participated by airing weekly clues. Each week the information led the listeners closer to the medallions' hiding places. The 20 winners didn't all use the same method in their searches. The historical nature of many of the clues tested the knowledge of the local treasure seekers. Some found the answers through research at the local library, while others simply pieced together the weekly clues which led them to the medallions.

What's a "break-open tournament"?

Q: What's a "break-open tournament"? I understand that state lotteries occasionally conduct them and some pretty great prizes are won.

A: Break-open tournaments are held in states that sell pull-tab games. These pull-tab lottery games, also called break-open or rip-off games, feature low-priced lottery tickets (25¢ to 50¢ each) that have several paper tabs to pull off which reveal play symbols on a line underneath. Players win by uncovering three matching symbols on any of the lines.

In a break-open tournament, the lottery uses advertising to invite players from around the state to join the tournament. On specific dates, preliminary rounds are held at taverns, restaurants and other locations where the break-open tickets are sold. Contestants race to remove as many tabs from the tickets as quickly as possible. Players win the cash that comes from matching three symbols.

In addition, the tickets used in these tournaments usually feature special bonus points under the tabs. The player who accumulates the most bonus points at each preliminary location moves on to the final competition at a later date. The final competition usually has additional grand prizes besides cash prizes. These tournaments are a lot of fun and they are very successful promotions for the lottery.

Which is easier to win: a 7-11-80 or 7-10-74 keno-type lotto game?

Q: I'm confused. I have a choice of playing two different keno-type lotto games run by two different state lotteries, but I don't know which has the better odds. One keno game has a 7-11-80 format and the other has a 7-10-74. Which one is easier to win? In both, I have to pick seven numbers correctly. In one game, the lottery draws 11 numbers out of a field of 80, and in the other 10 numbers are drawn out of a field of 74. Lowering the field from which you pick your numbers from 80 to 74 should make it easier to win, shouldn't it?

A: The 7-10-74 game is harder to win than the 7-11-80 game. Players pick seven numbers in both games, but by having the lottery select only 10 numbers instead of 11, it is less likely that you will have the correct seven numbers. The odds of hitting the jackpot in the 7-11-80 game are 9.6 million to one, while in the 7-10-74 game the odds are 14.9 million to one.

Are my chances of winning better with Powerball or with a 6/49 lotto?

Q: I live half the year in a state where we have a new Powerball game.pp13 In this game we have to correctly pick five numbers out of 45 plus one additional number out of another 45 numbers. Correctly picking these six numbers wins the jackpot. I think this is really like picking six numbers out of 90. I also live half the year in a state where the lotto game asks you to correctly pick six numbers out of 49. Although I don't know how to prove it, I think that my chances of winning the jackpot are better in the 6/49 game than in the 5/45-plus-1/45 game. Can you tell me the difference in the odds of winning the jackpot for these two games?

A: You are absolutely right. It's much tougher to win the grand prize in Powerball than in the 6/49 lotto. Your chances of having the correct six numbers in the 6/49 game are 1 in 14 million. Your chances of having the correct six numbers in the new Powerball game are 1 in 55 million. A big difference! Isn't it interesting that all of a sudden your chances of winning in the 6/49 game don't look so bad anymore?

When is our lottery going to give away merchandise prizes?

Q: When is our state lottery going to offer games that give away merchandise prizes as well as money? My sister lives in Idaho, and the state lottery there frequently offers games where players can win some really neat merchandise prizes as well as money.

A: As long as games which only offer money as prizes are doing well, lottery officials don't particularly like to offer cash-

and-merchandise games. Offering lottery games which award significant merchandise as well as money is always more work for lottery officials and costs the lottery more money than games that don't offer gift prizes. In addition, it seems that players like the games with merchandise prizes better than the games that simply offer cash prizes. Consequently, the public pressures the lottery to keep offering merchandise games once the first cash-and-merchandise game is offered.

The Idaho Lottery that your sister plays is a good example of a state lottery that offers frequent cash-and-merchandise games. In one game, the Idaho Lottery offered a scratch-off game called "BUCKS'N'TRUCKS II." It was the second game by the same name that not only gave players the chance to win money but also to win one of several 1992 Ford XLT SuperCab pickups if their instant game ticket had three trucks on it when it was scratched. This game was so popular the first time the lottery offered it, and there were so many player requests for it to be repeated, the lottery made arrangements to offer it again.

One problem with merchandise games like this when they are offered in any lottery state is that players have a tendency to ignore the other scratch-off games and spend most of their money on the merchandise game. Idaho had 12 other current instant games besides "BUCKS'N'TRUCKS." Sales of tickets for those other games suffered until "BUCKS'N'TRUCKS" was sold out.

Index

N

O

P

Best Bets from Bonus Books

Break the One-Armed Bandits
How to come out ahead when you play the slots
Frank Scoblete
ISBN 1-56625-001-3 • 178 pages • paper • $9.95

Beat the Craps out of the Casinos
How to play craps and win
Frank Scoblete
ISBN 0-929387-34-1 • 152 pages • paper • $9.95

Guerrilla Gambling
How to beat the casinos—game by game
Frank Scoblete
ISBN 1-56625-027-7 • 339 pages • paper • $12.95

Workouts and Maidens
Inside betting info for those who want to win at the track
Vincent Reo
ISBN 1-56625-000-5 • 180 pages • paper • $11.95

Finding HOT Horses
Pick horses that can win for you
Vincent Reo
ISBN 0-929387-96-1 • 135 pages • paper • $12.00

Overlay, Overlay: How to Bet Horses Like a Pro
Leading trainers and jockeys share their handicapping secrets
Bill Heller
ISBN 0-933893-86-8 • 228 pages • paper • $9.95

Harness Overlays: Beat the Favorite
We'll show you how
Bill Heller
ISBN 0-929387-97-X • 139 pages • paper • $12.00

Woulda, Coulda, Shoulda
"Best introduction to horse racing ever written"—*Thoroughbred Times*
Dave Feldman with Frank Sugano
ISBN 0-933893-02-3 • 281 pages • paper • $9.95

Bonus Books, Inc., 160 East Illinois Street, Chicago, Illinois 60611

TOLL-FREE: 800 • 225 • 3775   **FAX: 312 • 467 • 9271**